I hope you enjoy colouring these greyscale illustrations which have been inspired by a fruit garden.

I and the Engaged in Art Community would love to see how you colour the fruit illustrations and you are invited to send a scan or photo of your finished colourings via e-mail to lesley@engagedinart.com for inclusion in our galleries.

I would also like to invite you to join the "Colouring and Tangling" private Group on Facebook where you can post your colourings and meet a friendly, creative and non-judgemental virtual community at https://www.facebook.com/groups/colouringandtangling/

Disclaimer

Fruit Garden - an Adult Colouring Book © Lesley Smitheringale

Bonus free Colouring Guide

The Fruit Garden illustrations can be coloured any way you choose but if you wish to take on the challenge of making the fruit look good enough to eat and realistic by using tonal blends, I have prepared a pdf booklet in full colour for owners of the "Fruit Garden" to download to your computer. It is a step-by-step guide of colouring cherries using colour pencils and the practice sheet included in the book. Also included are 9 finished example colourings from the Fruit Garden Book to inspire you. This private link is for you only and must not be shared.

http://www.engagedinart.com/coloring_cherries_from_the_fruit_garden_book_eia/

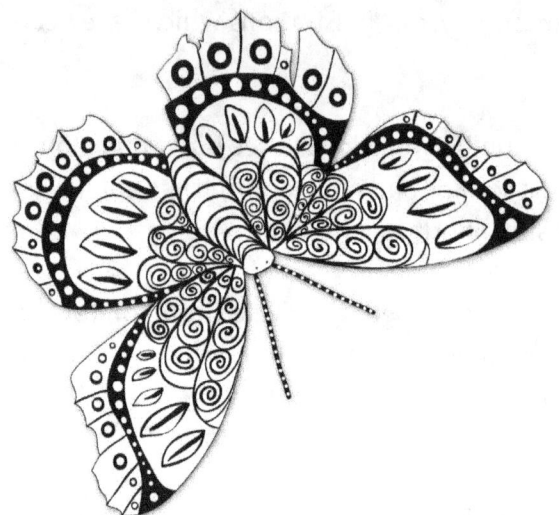

About the Artist

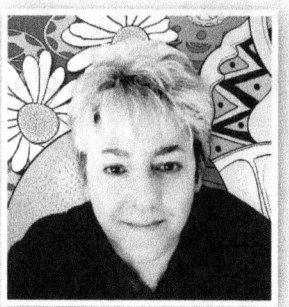

Lesley Smitheringale

Lesley lives and works in her home studio in the Redlands area of Queensland, Australia. She was born in Glasgow, Scotland where she obtained a BA with honours in Design at Glasgow School of Art. She then did further training to become an art teacher and after teaching for twenty years to Middle and High School students, Lesley took the plunge and decided to work for herself. She currently produces her own artwork where she embraces both traditional and digital media.

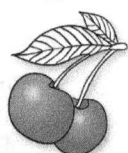

Lesley produces a range of hand-made, nature inspired giftware in her Oz Wildlife Studio Shop and also provides art and craft resources on her Engaged in Art Website where she acts as a "virtual" art teacher, sharing the techniques and creative ideas she has learned on her art journey.

Lesley also runs a private Group on Facebook called "Colouring and Tangling" where she provides a virtual meeting place for adults who love to colour and produce zentangle-inspired artworks.

She also runs workshops for adults in her home studio "Tea & Tangling" and "Coffee & Colouring" for those who live in the Brisbane|Redlands area of Queensland.

www.ozwildlifestudio.com
www.engagedinart.com

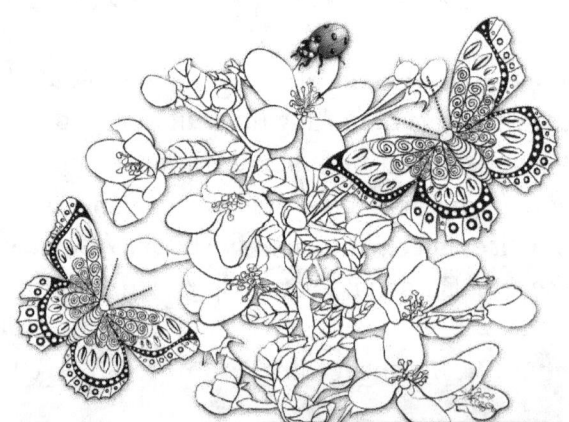

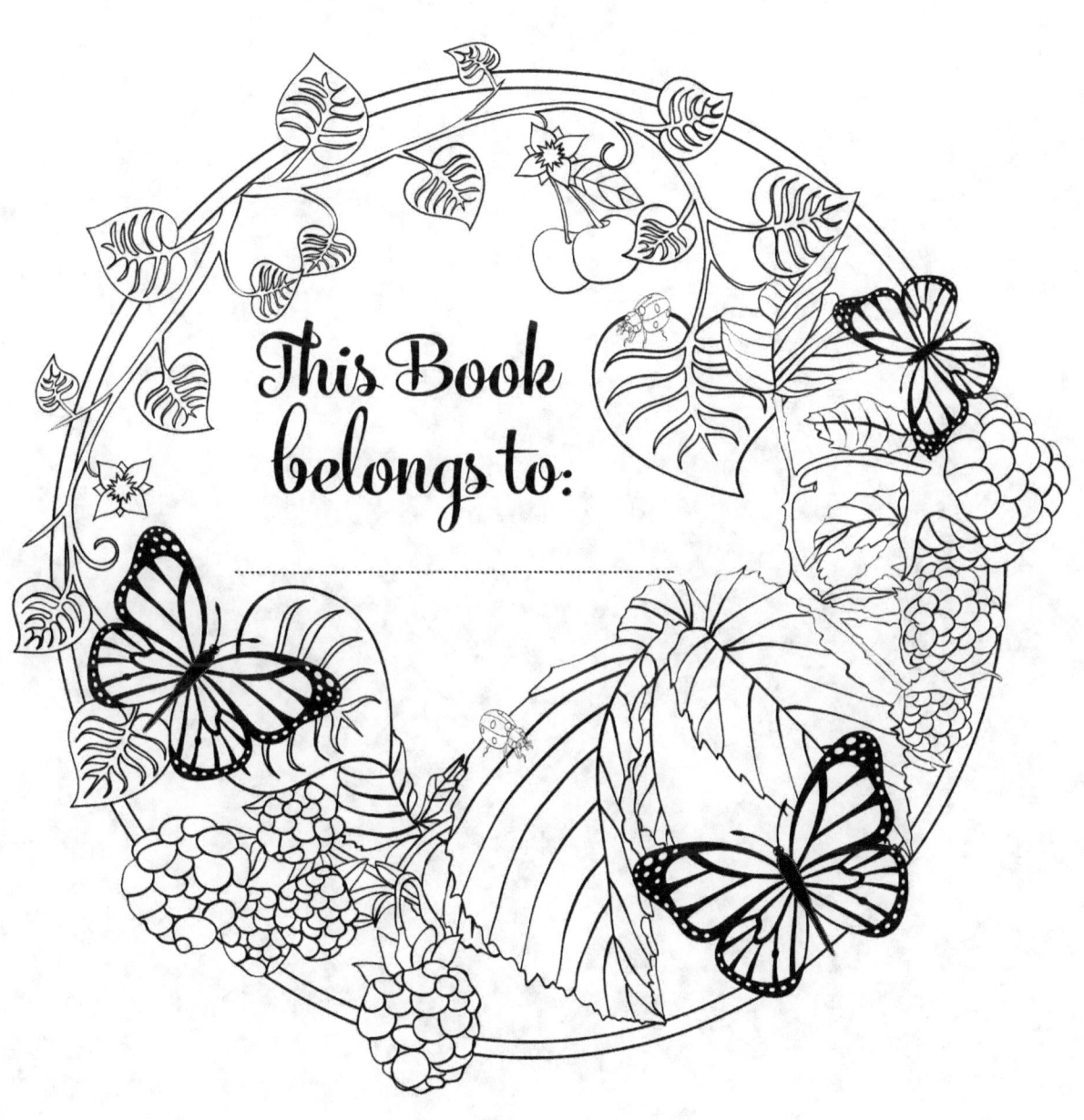

This Book
belongs to:

_____

Practice Sheet

Here are some separate fruits where
you can practise your colouring.

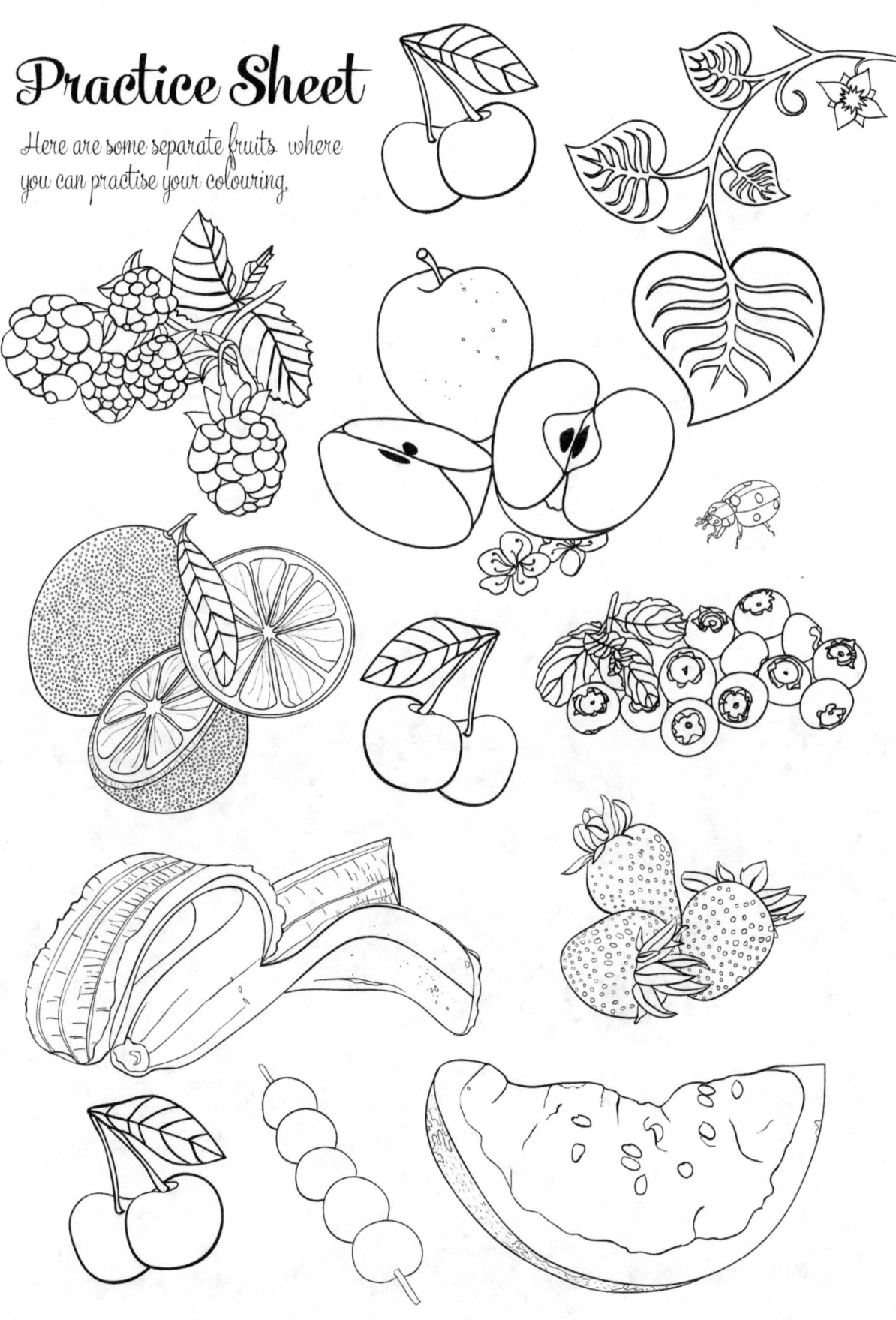

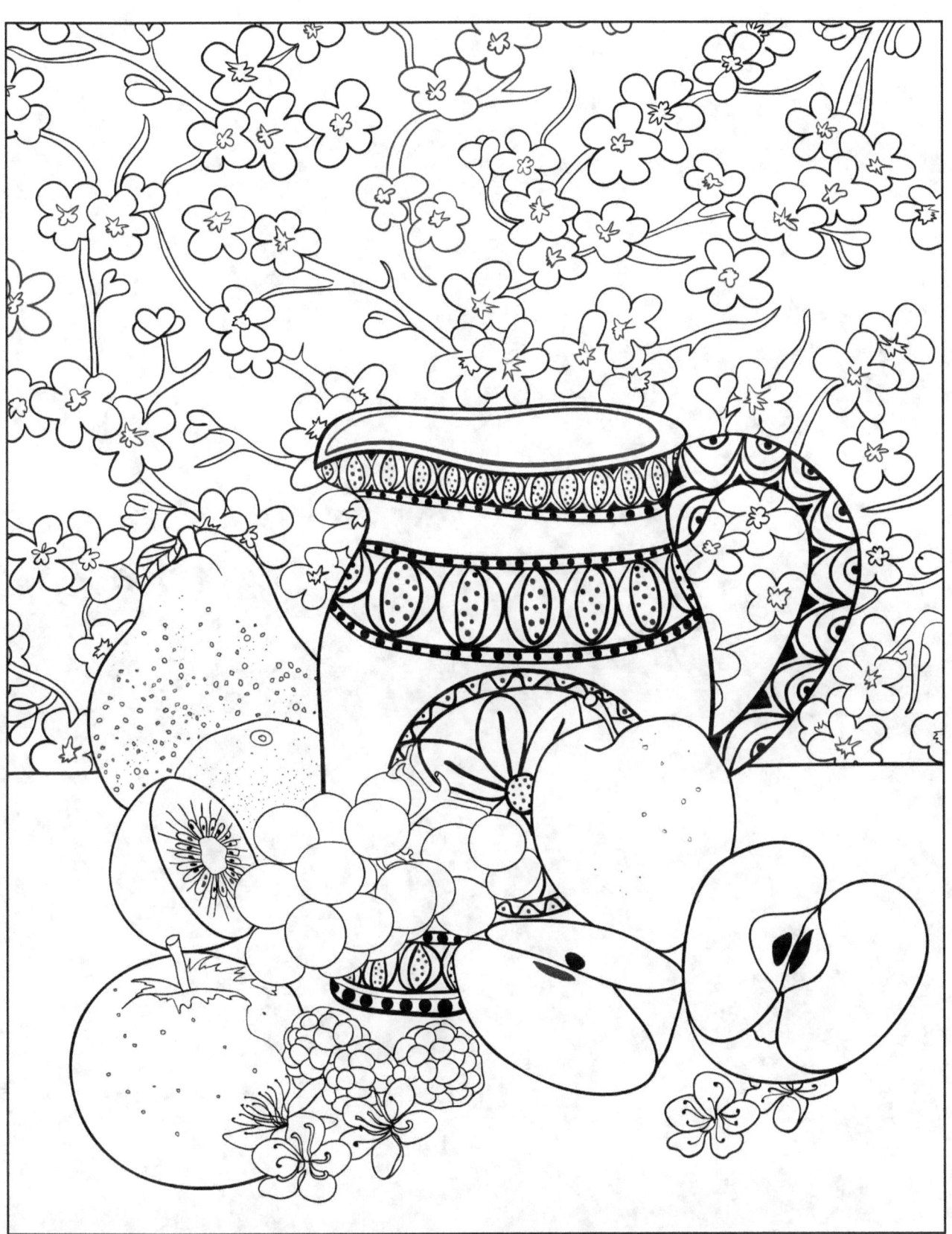

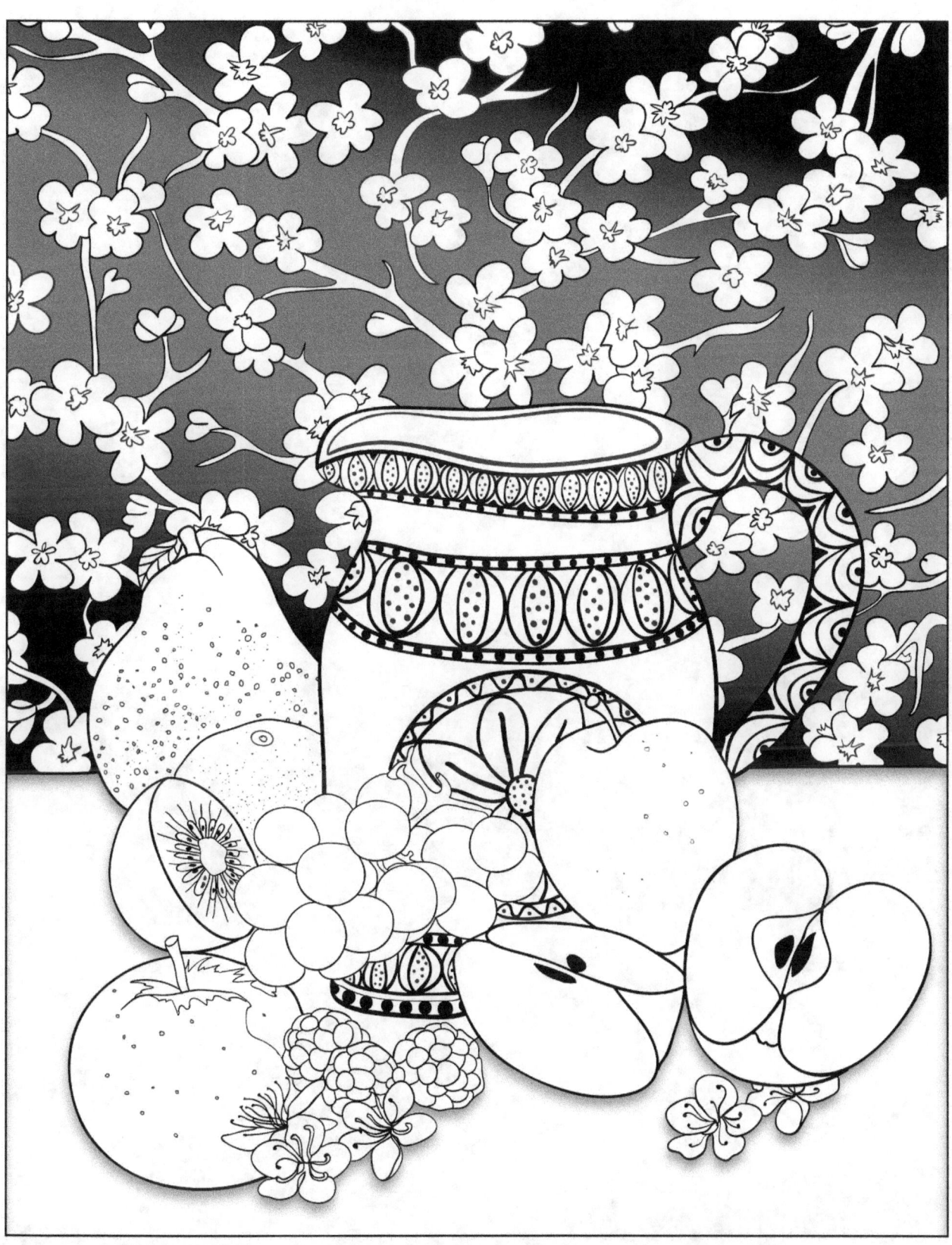

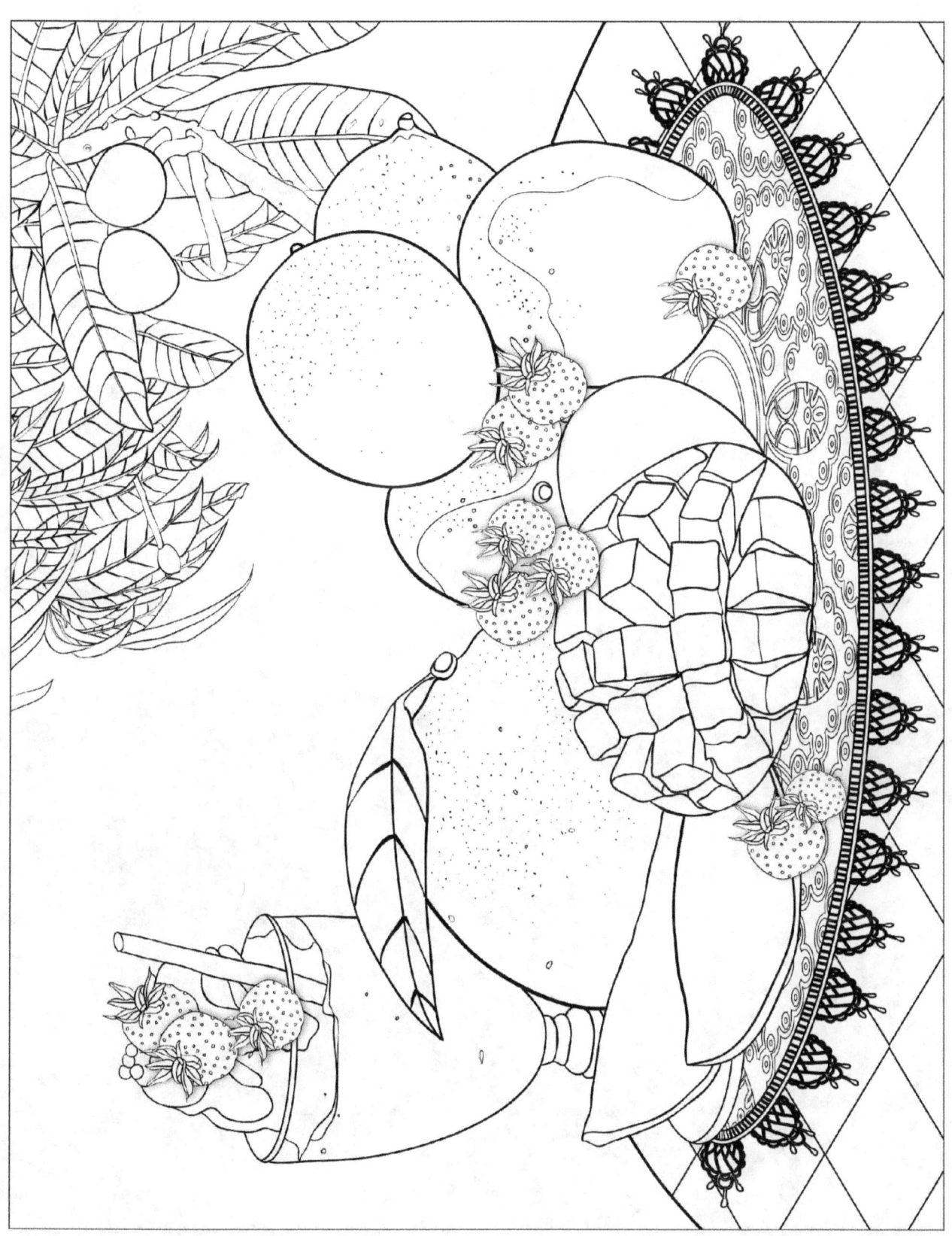

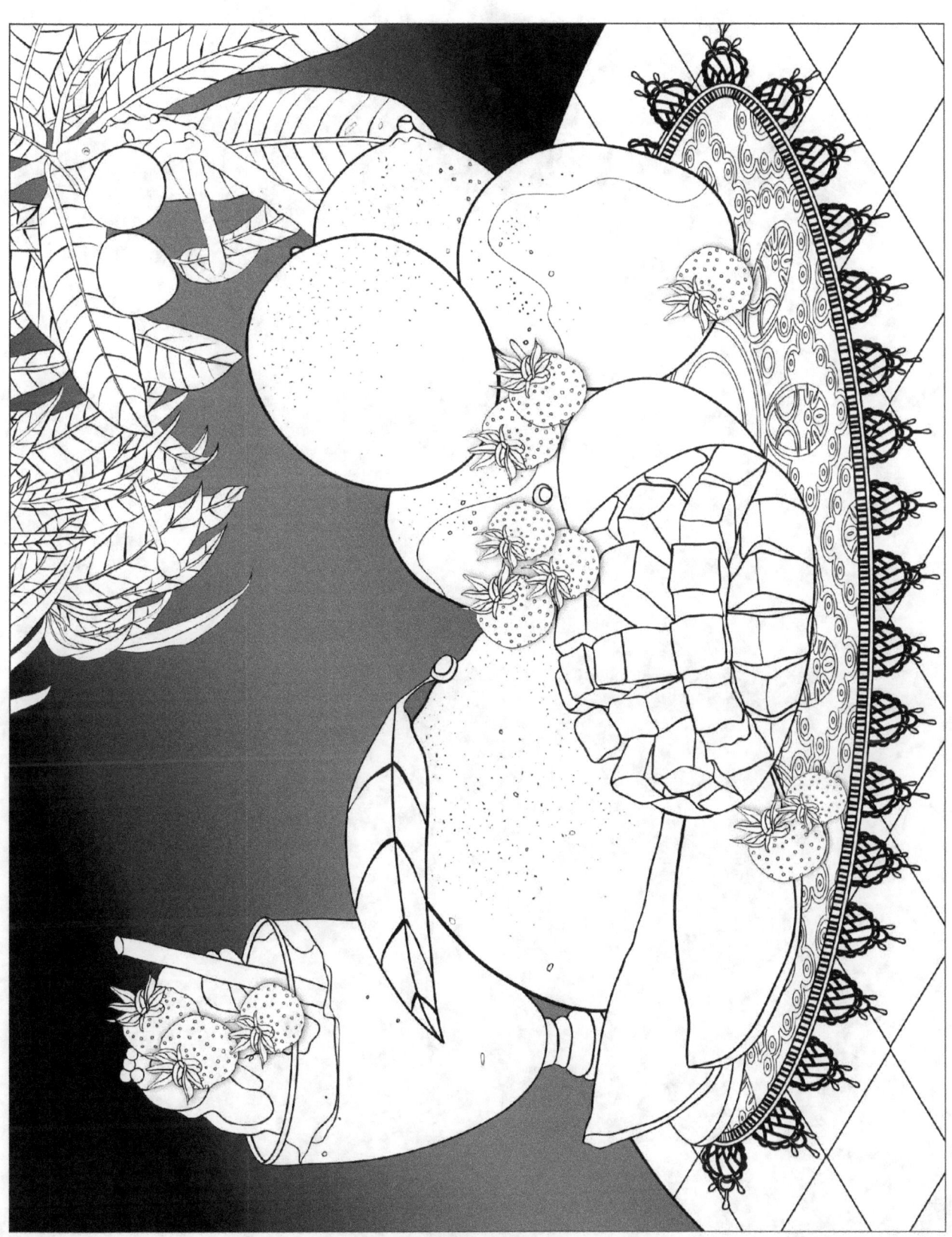

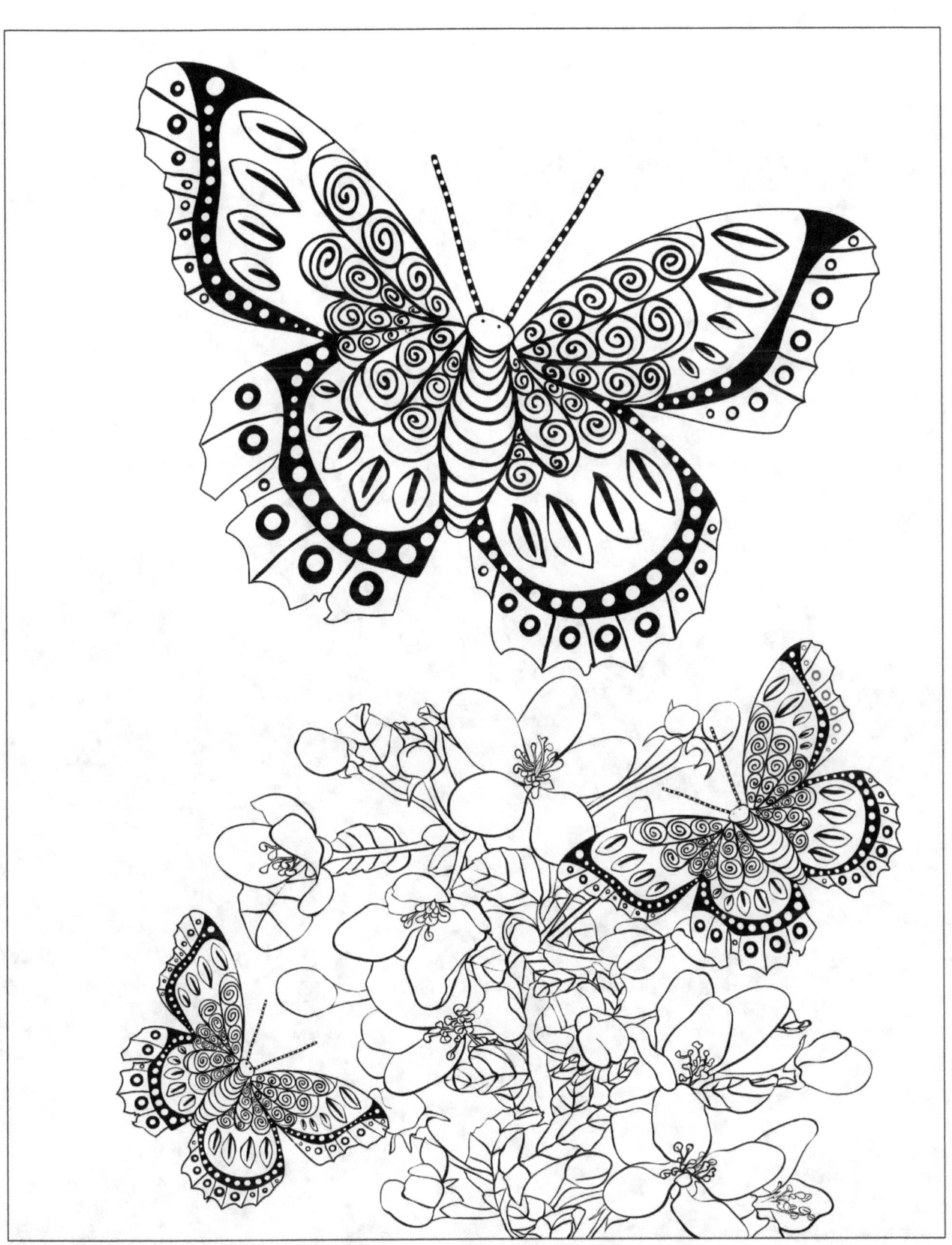

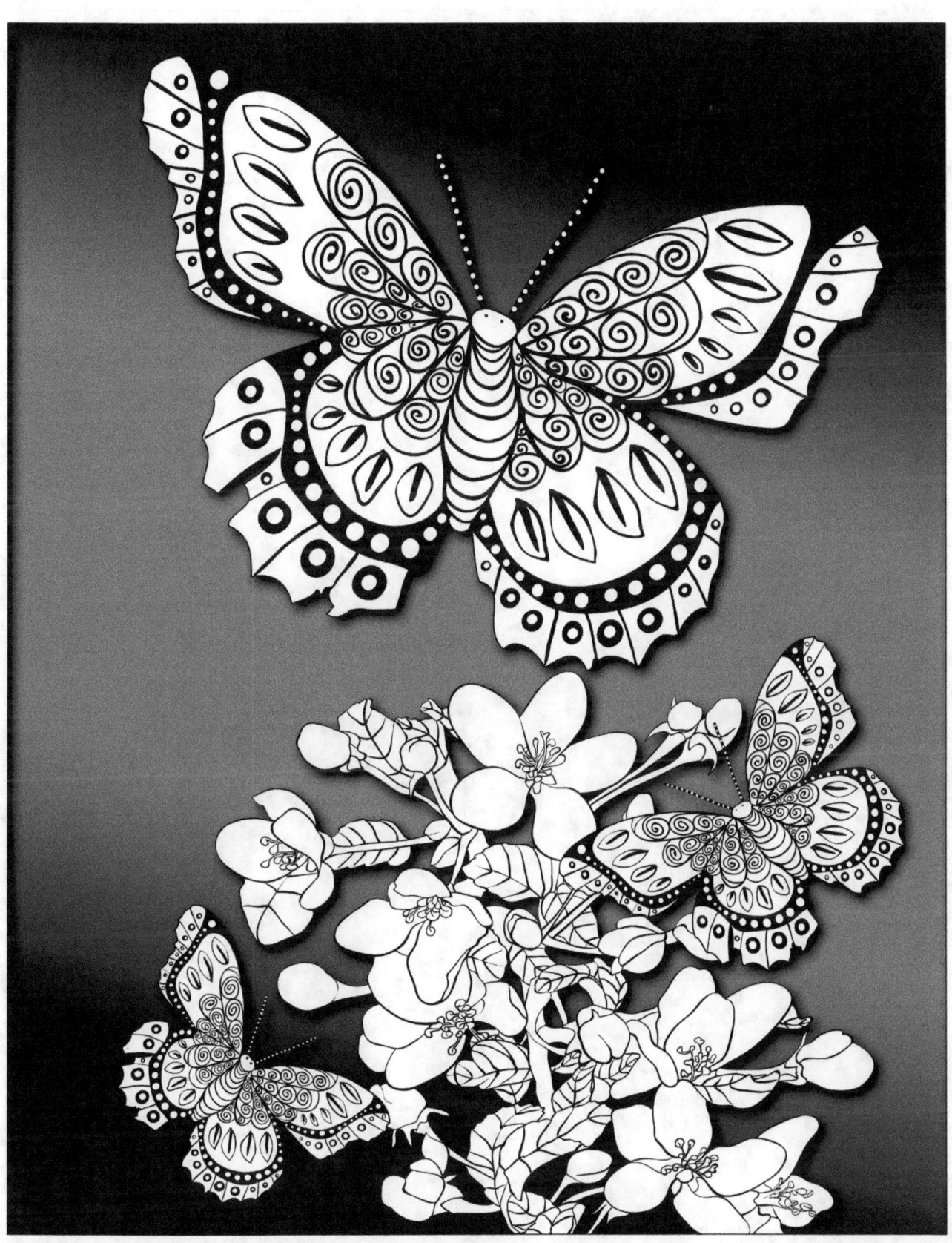

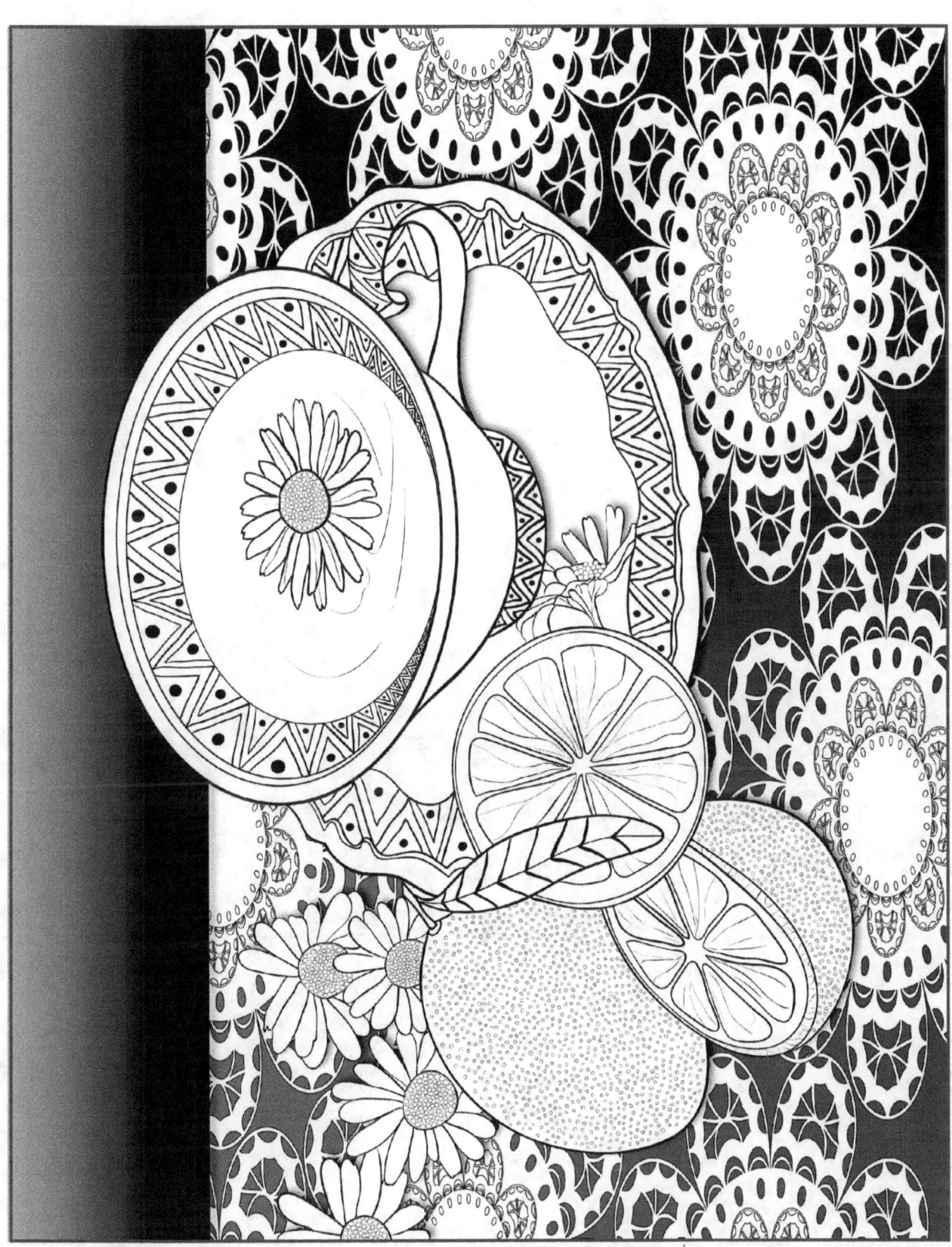

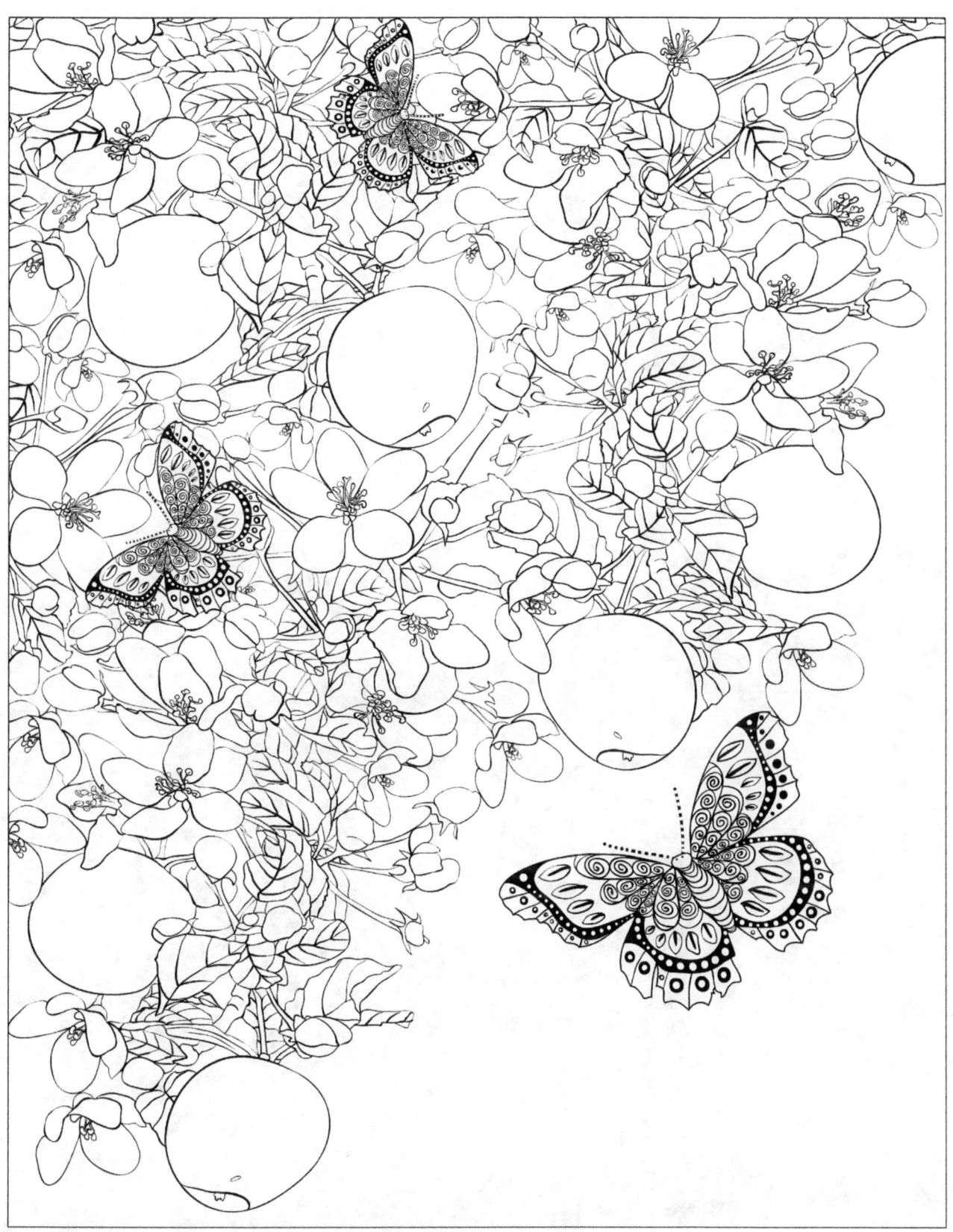

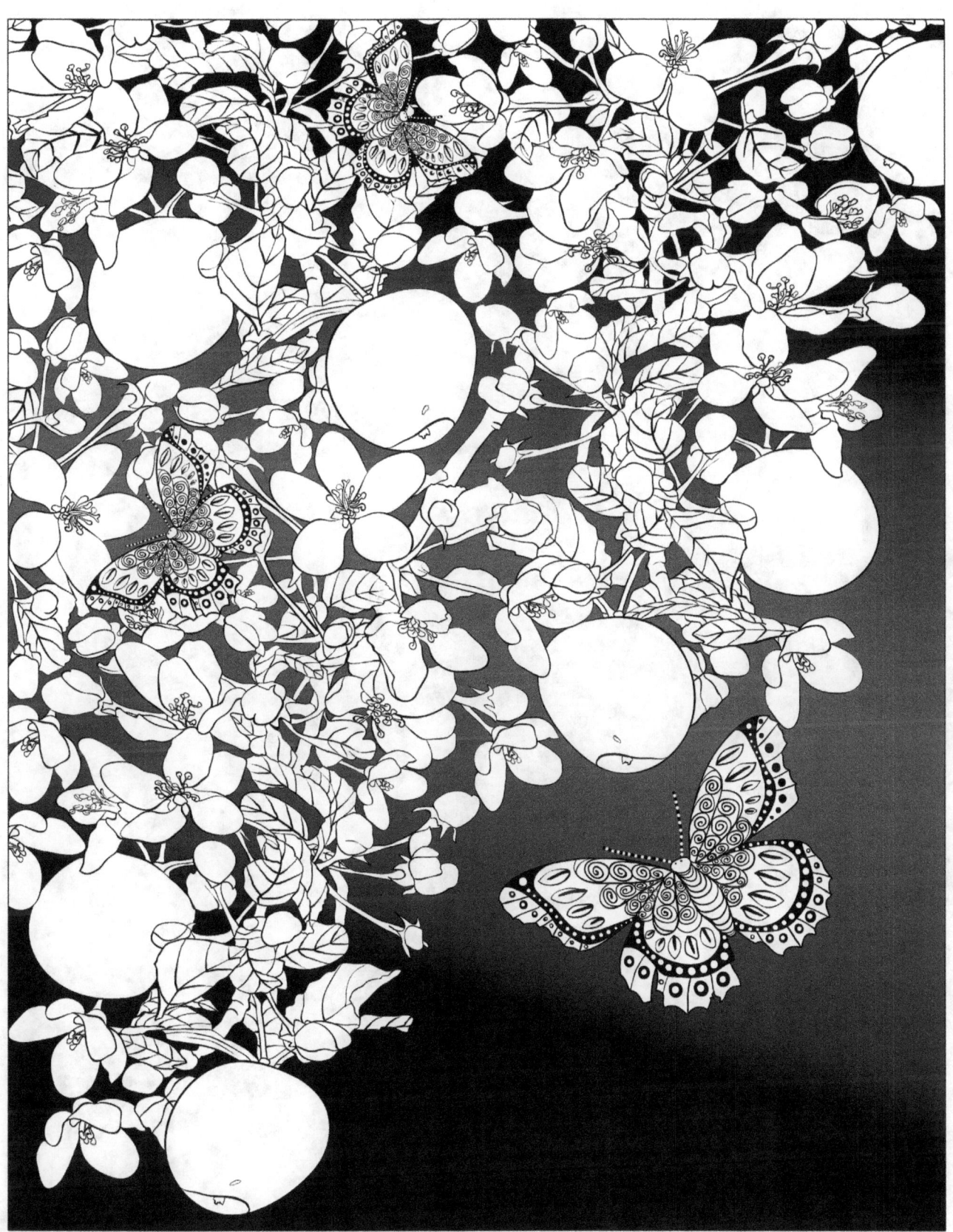

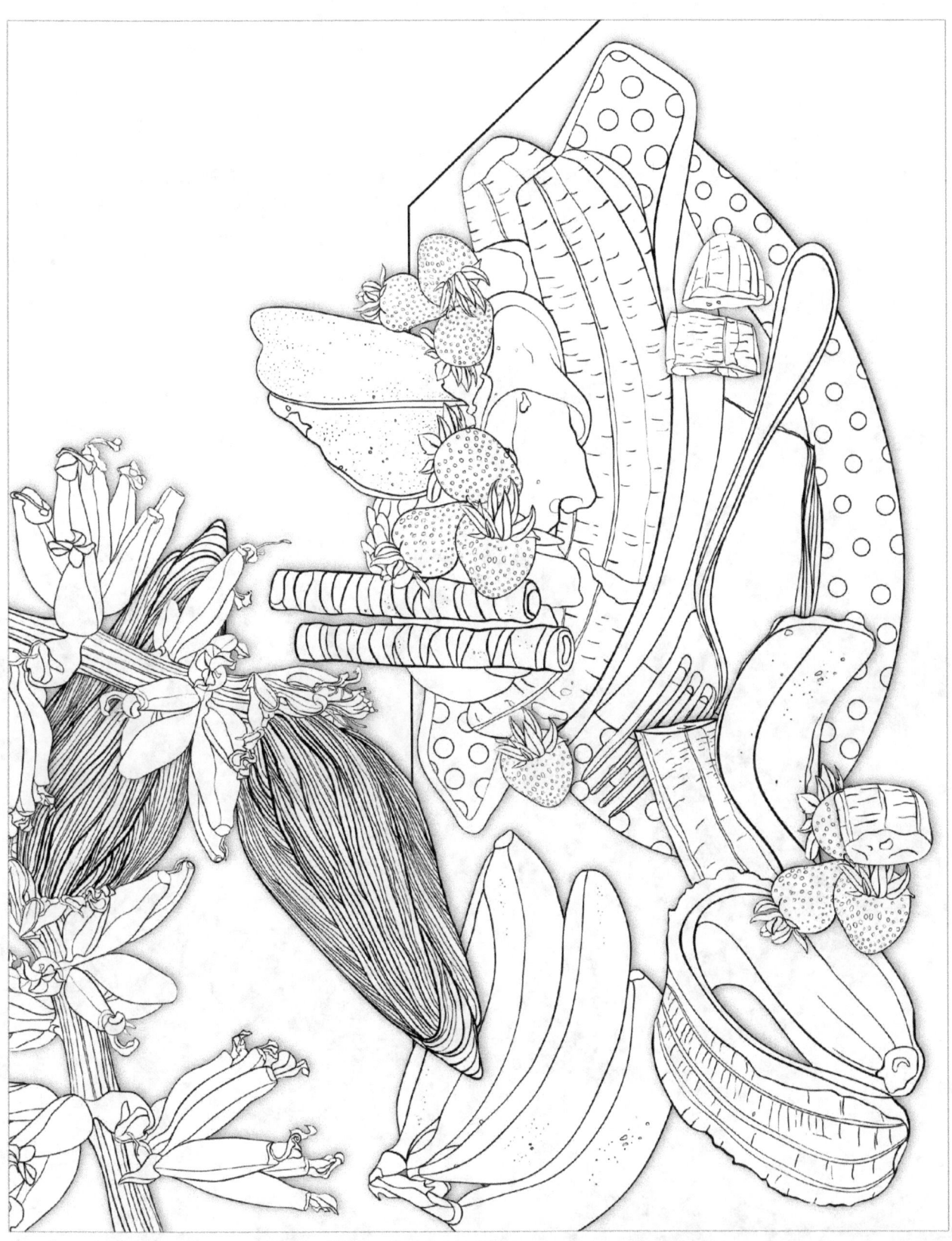

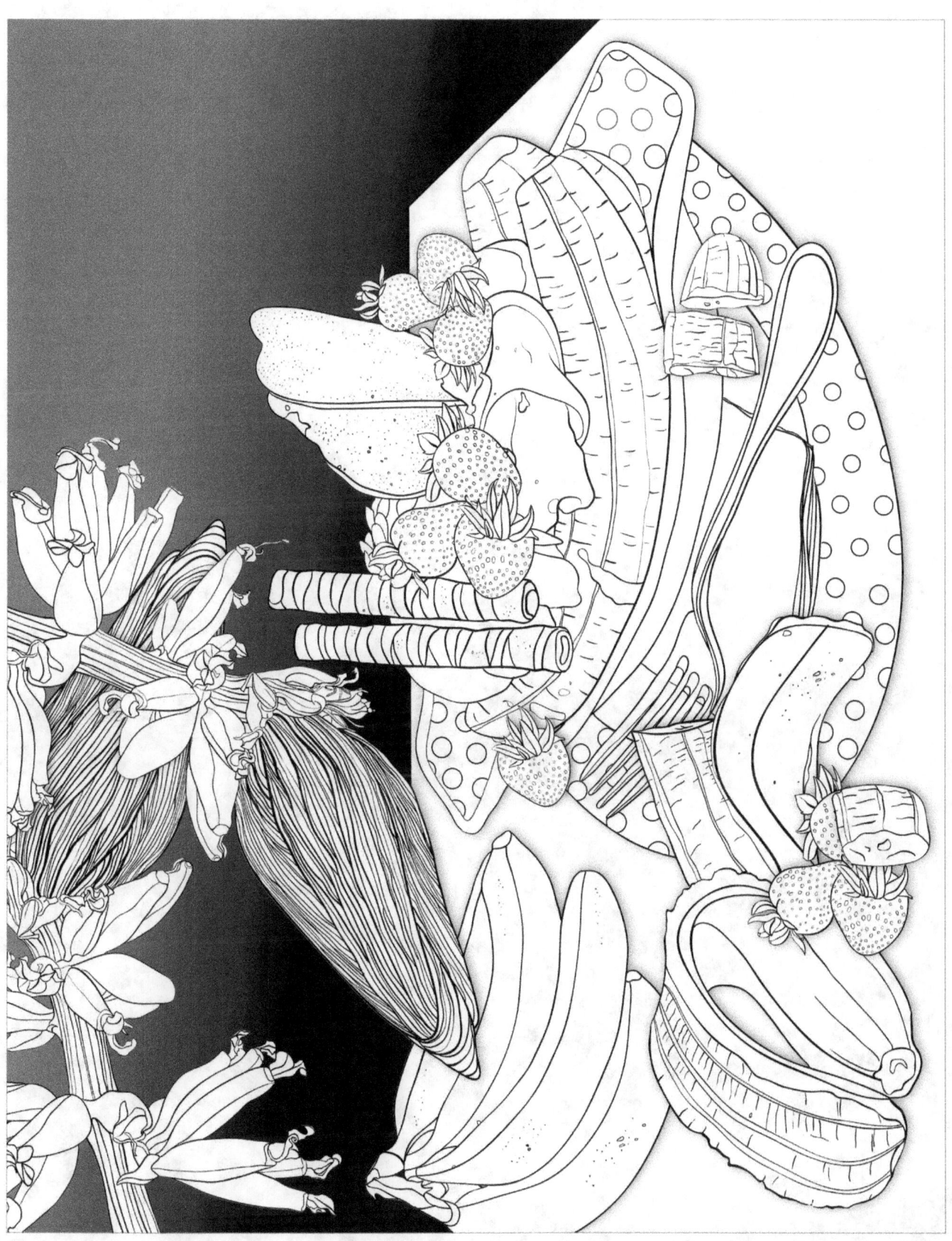

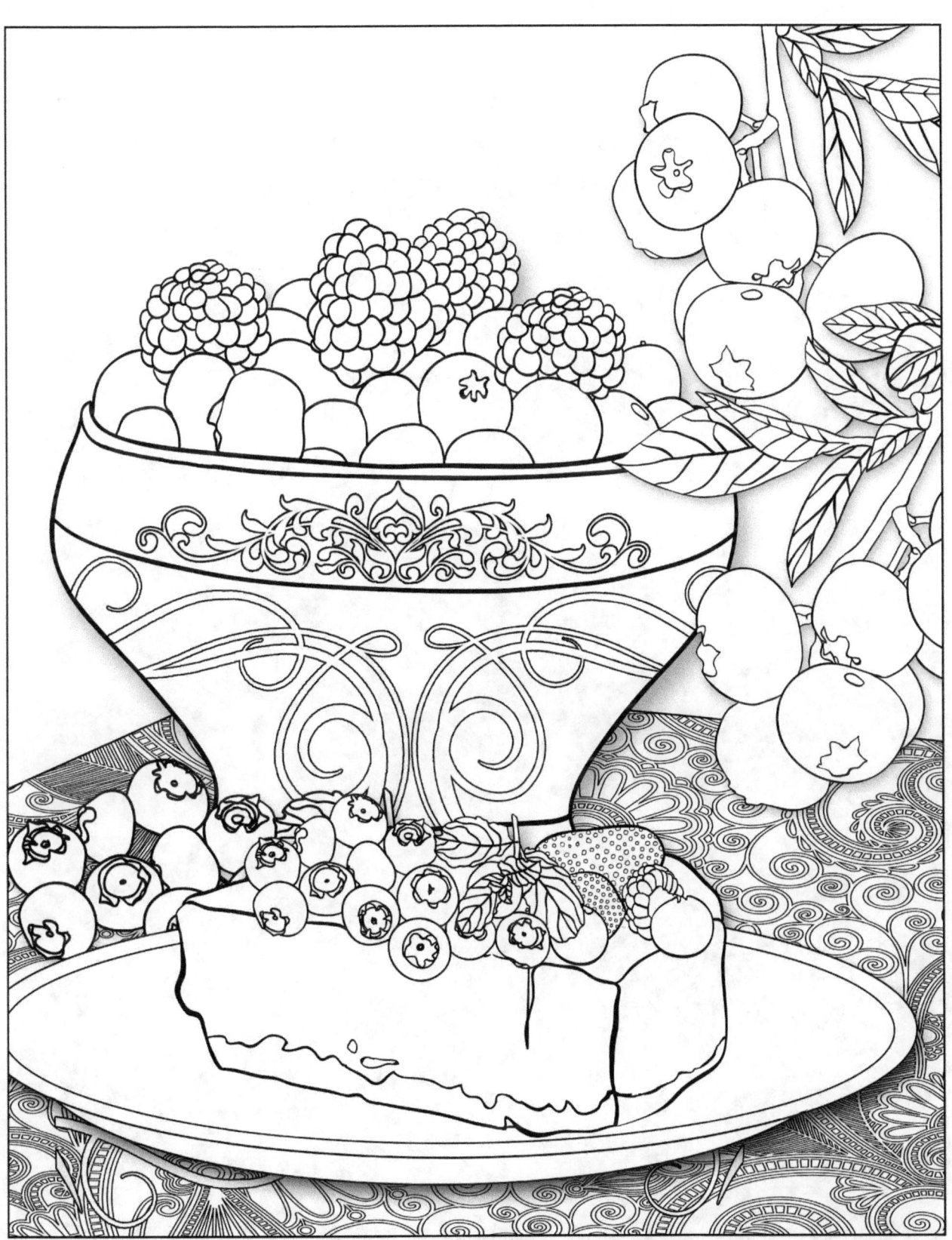

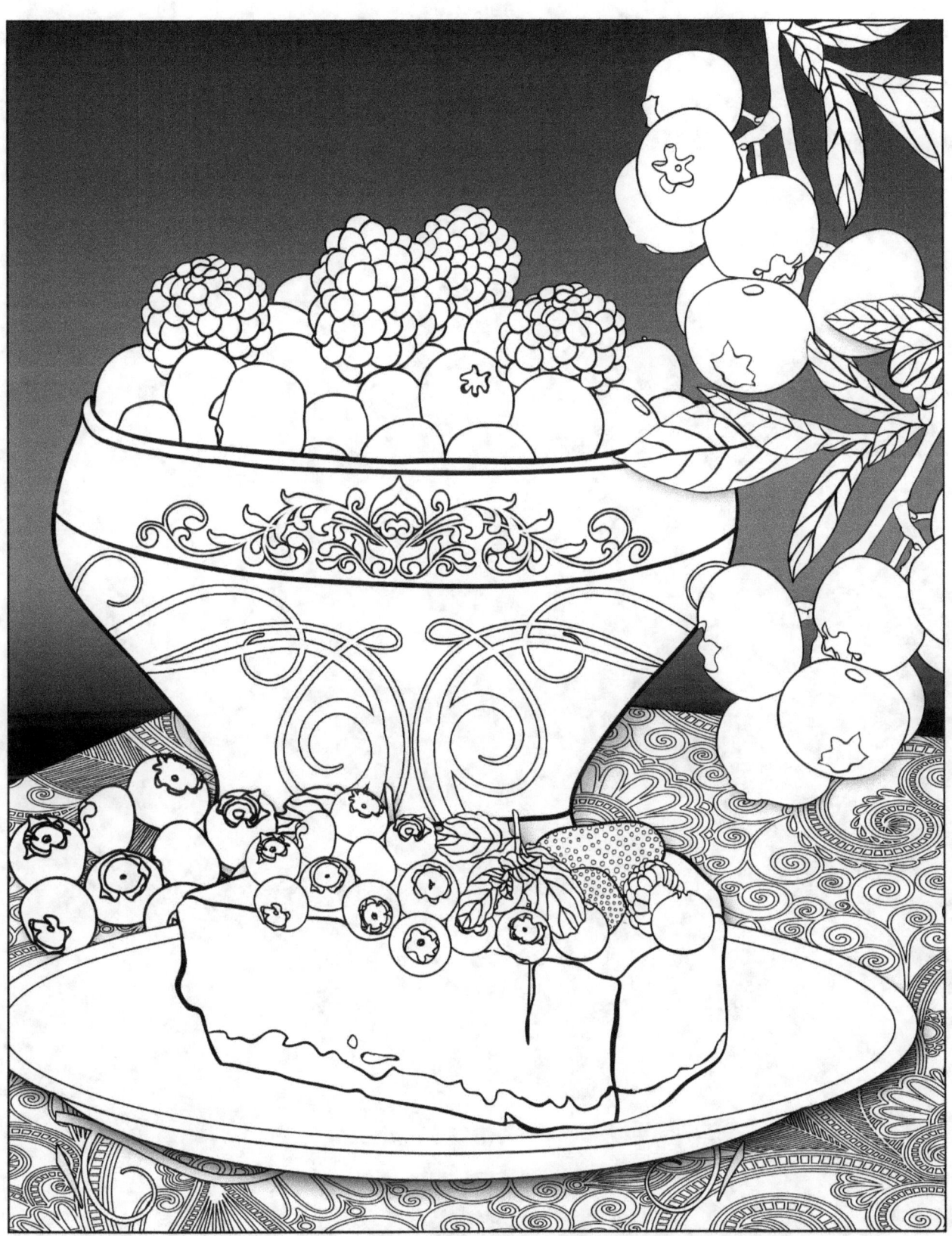

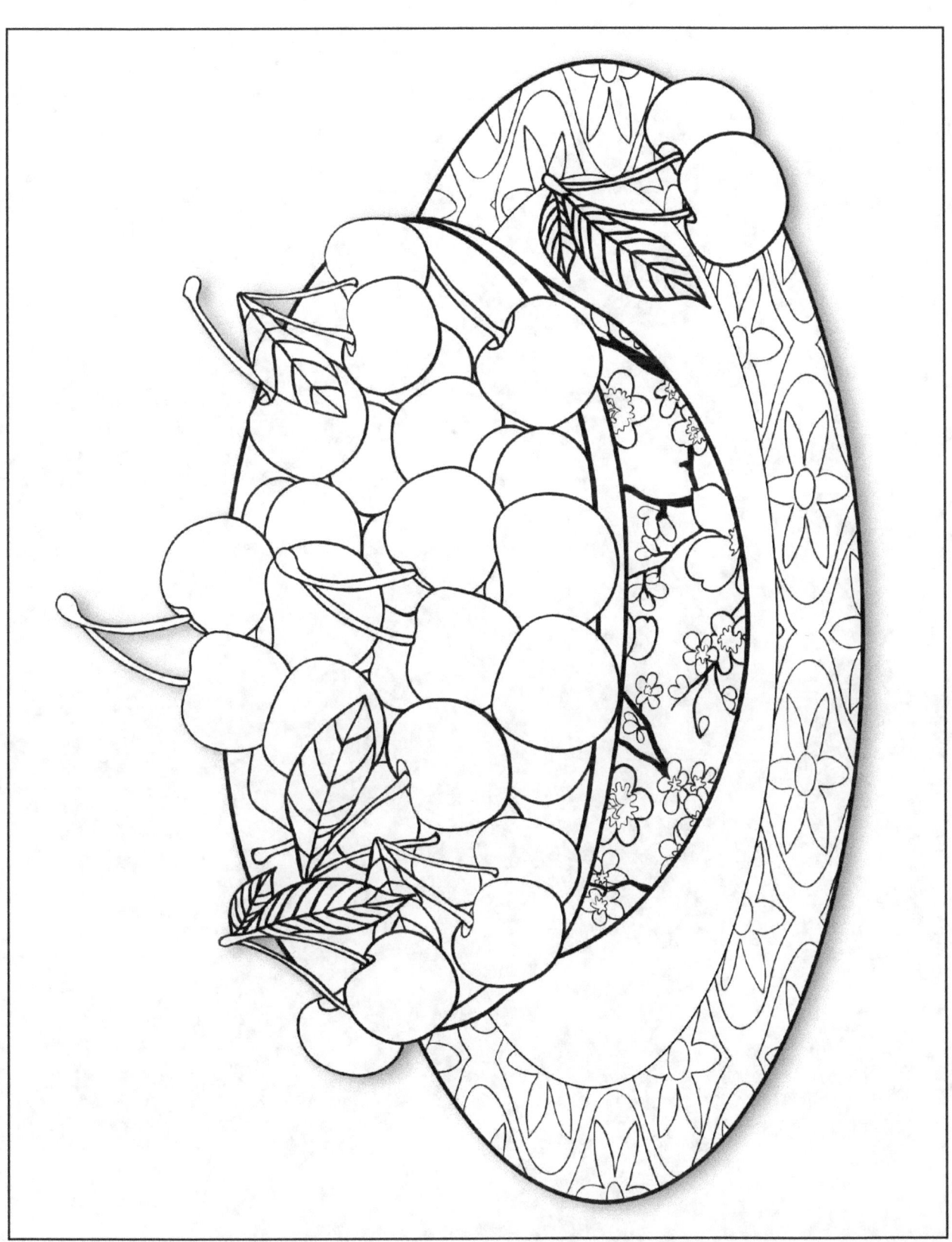

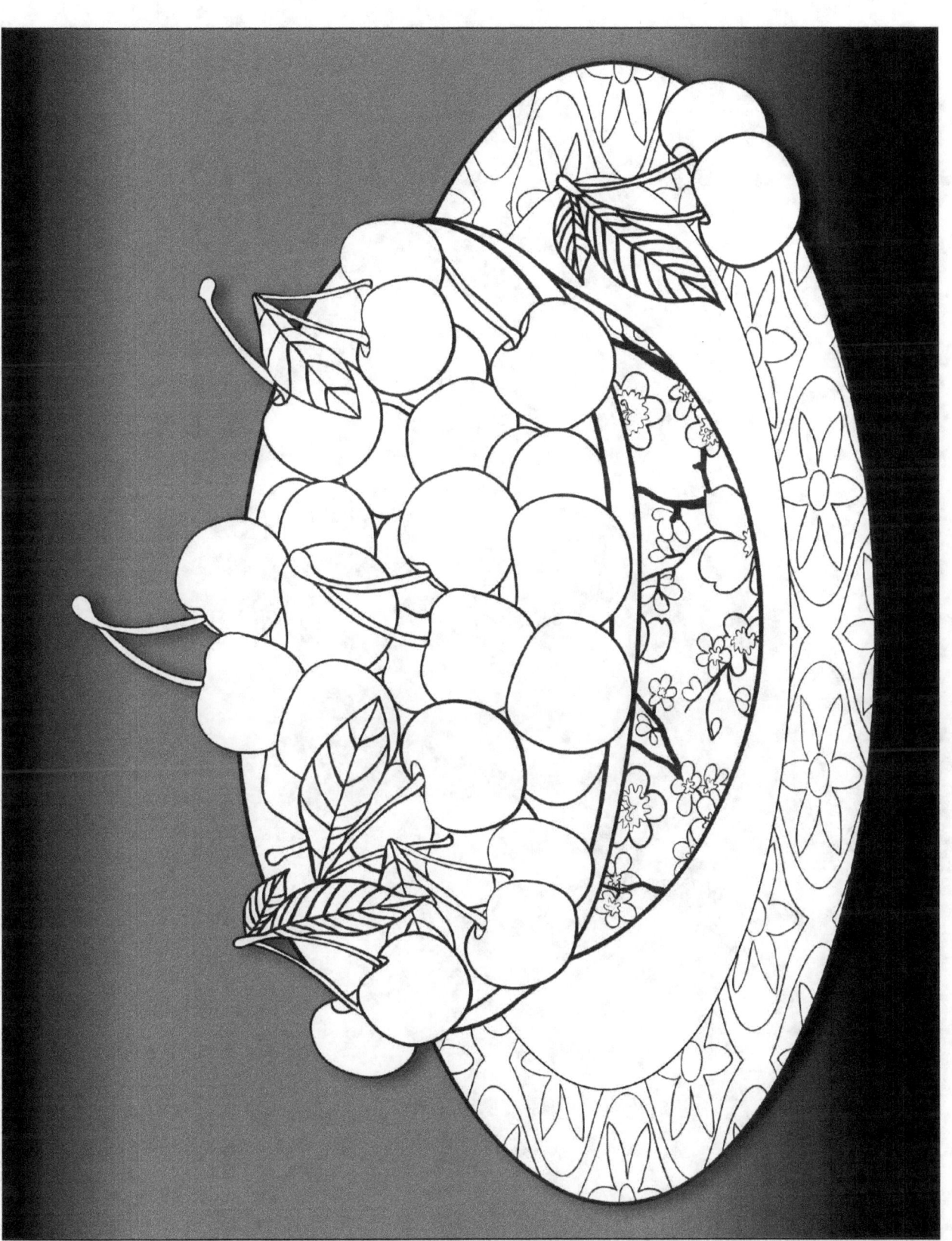

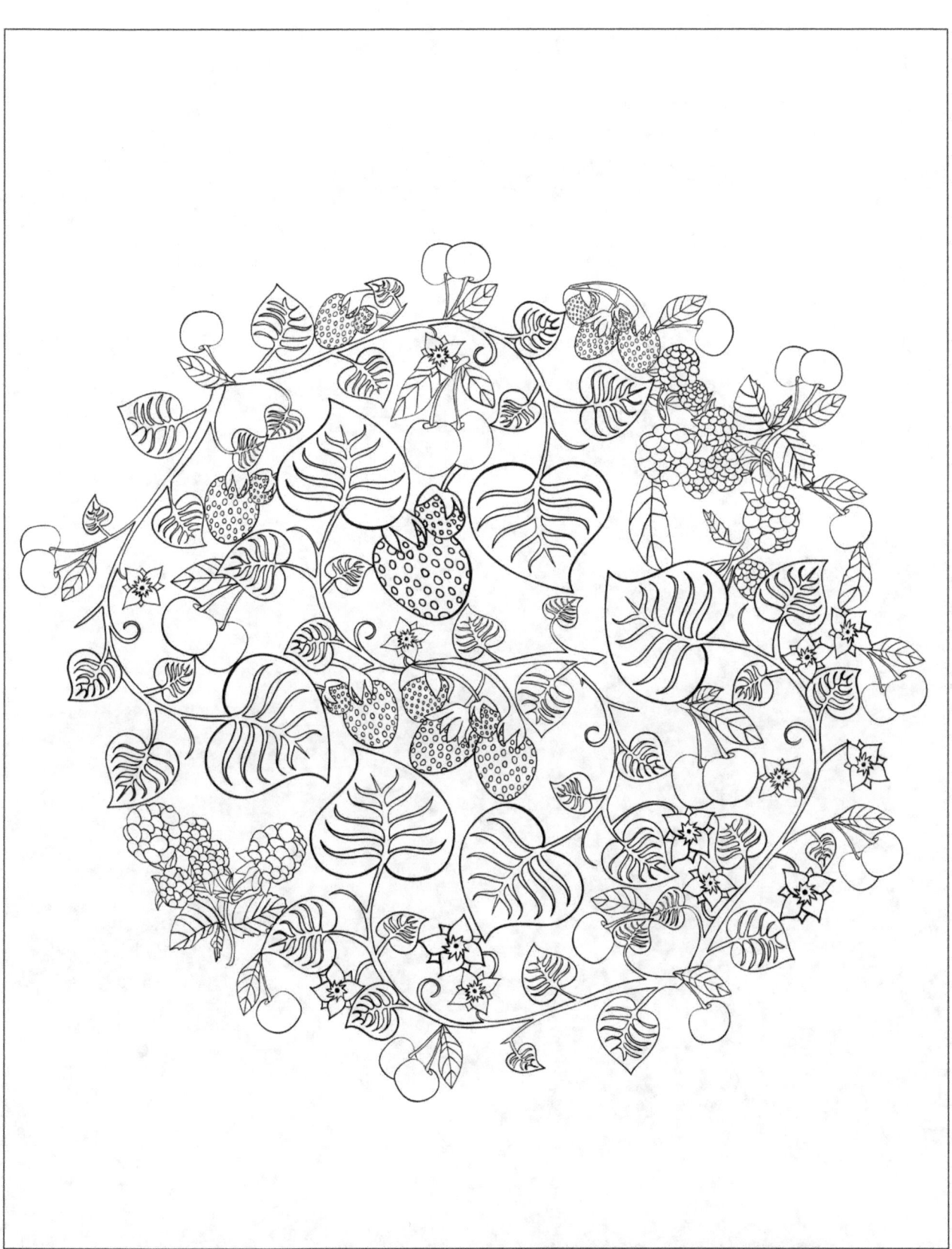

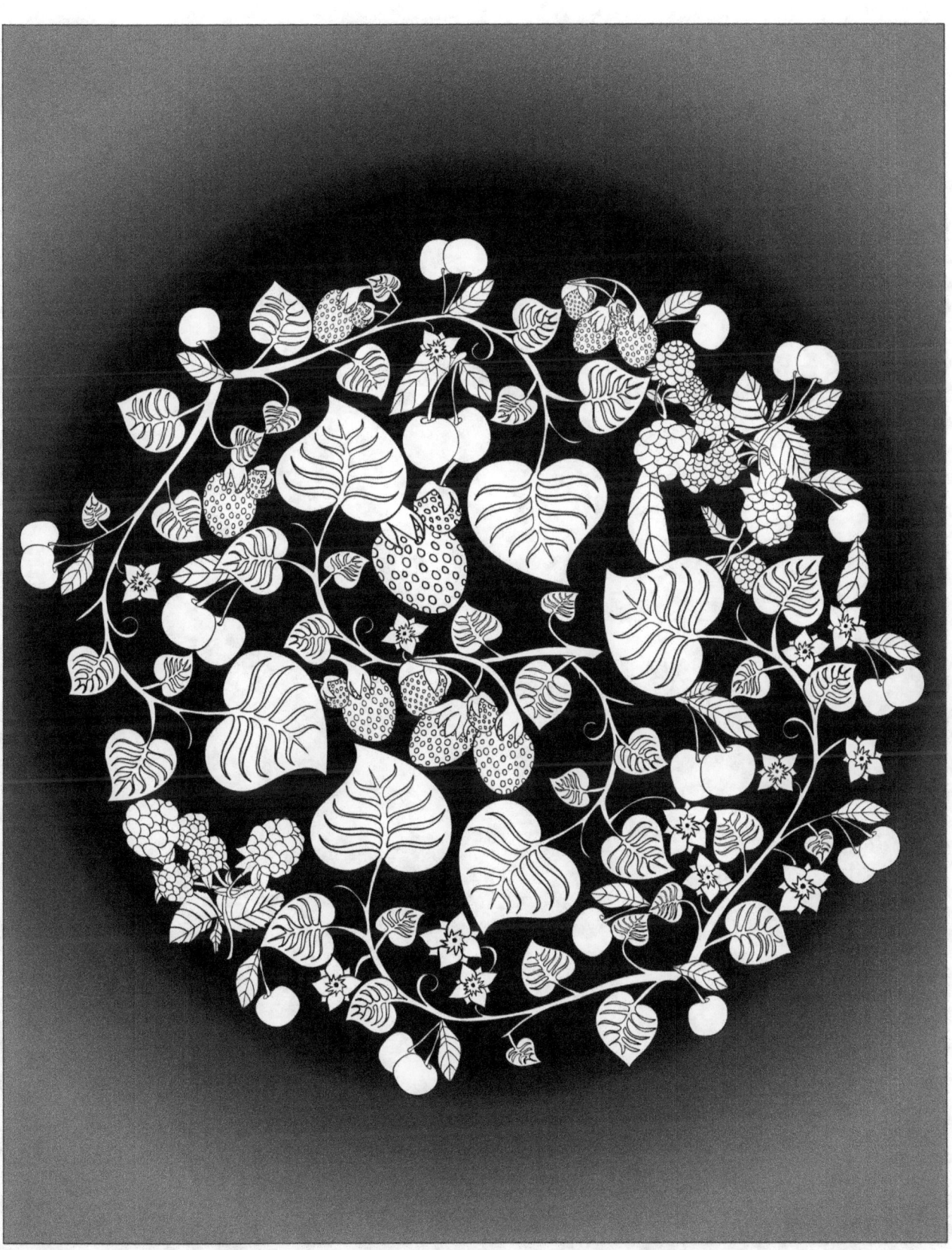

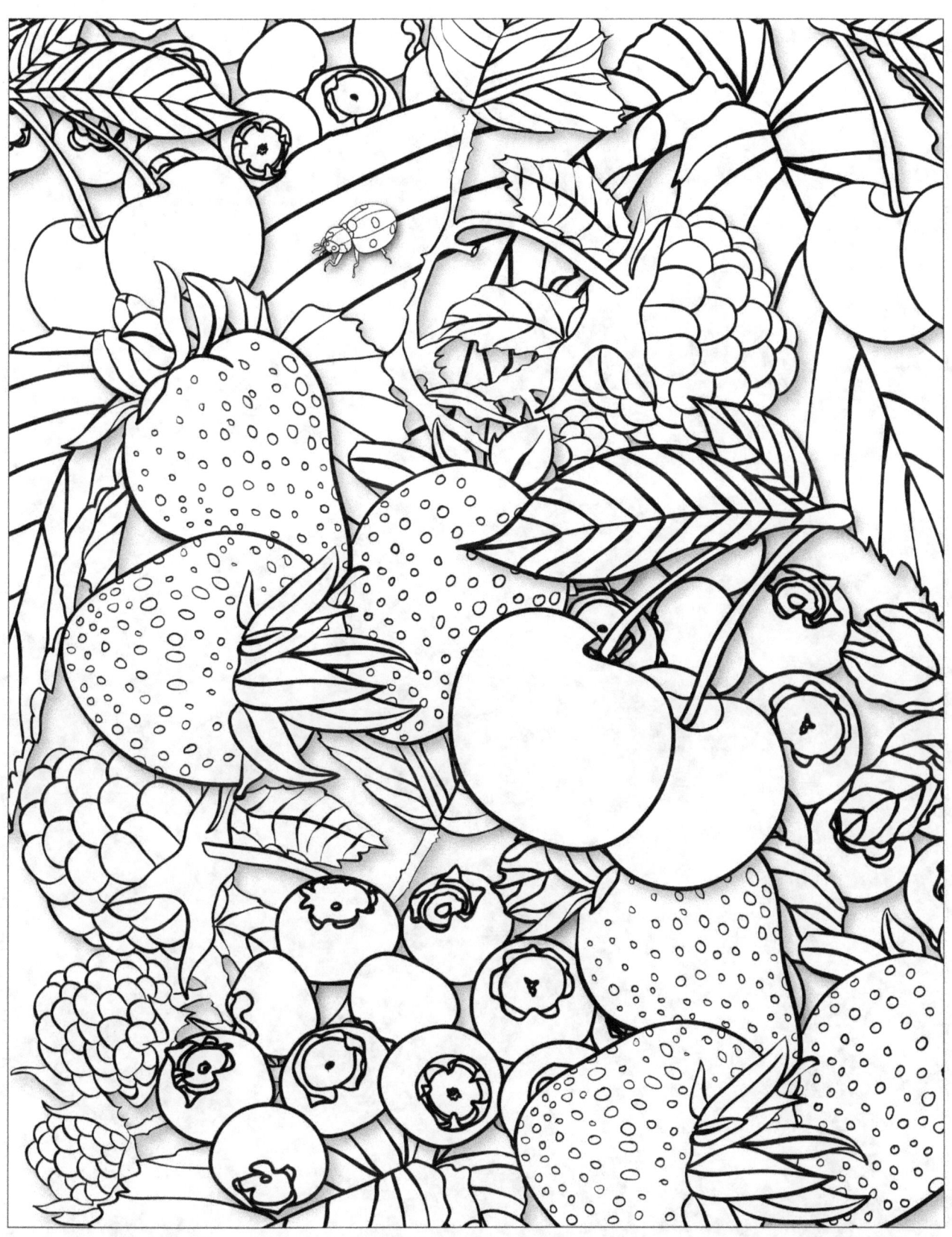

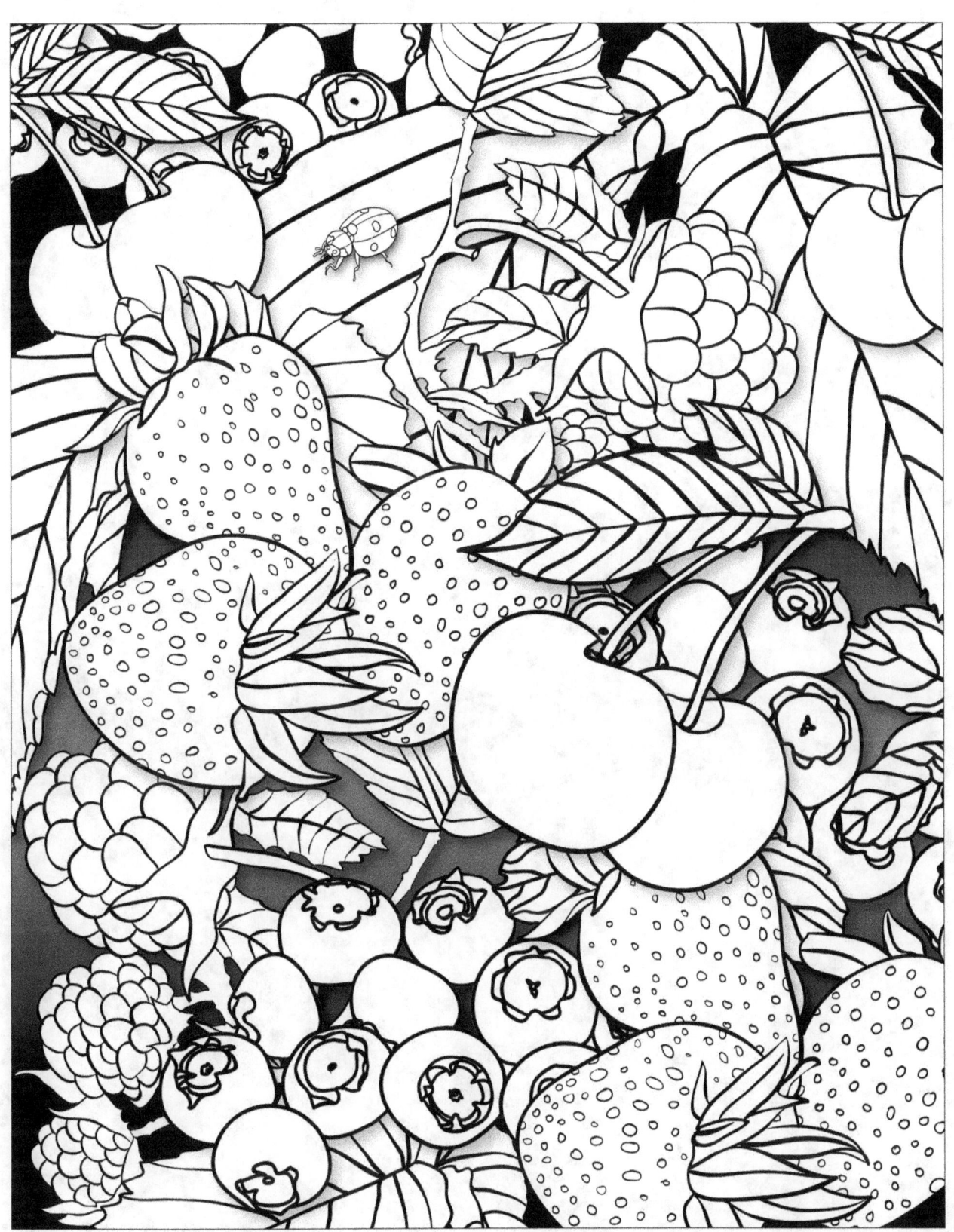

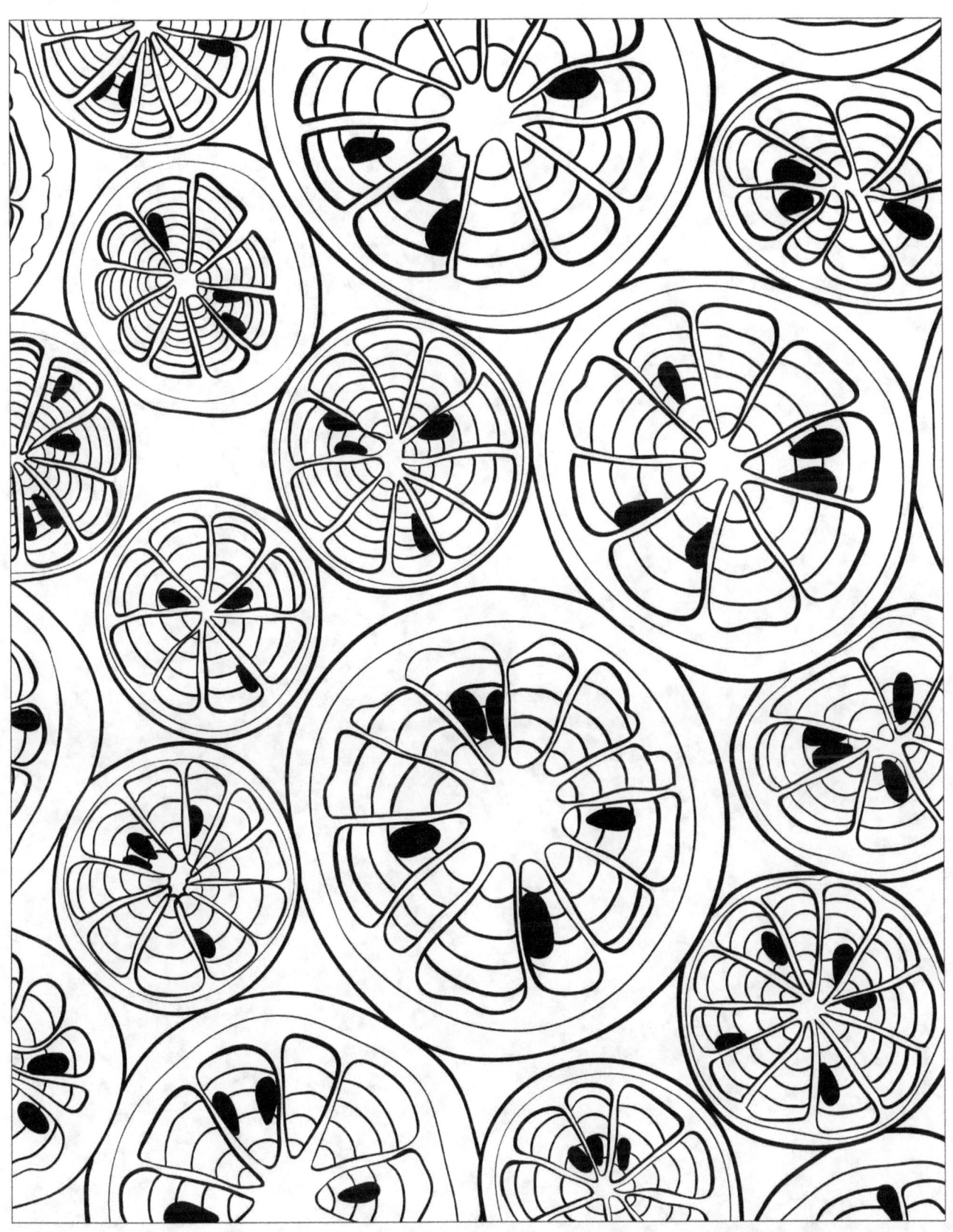

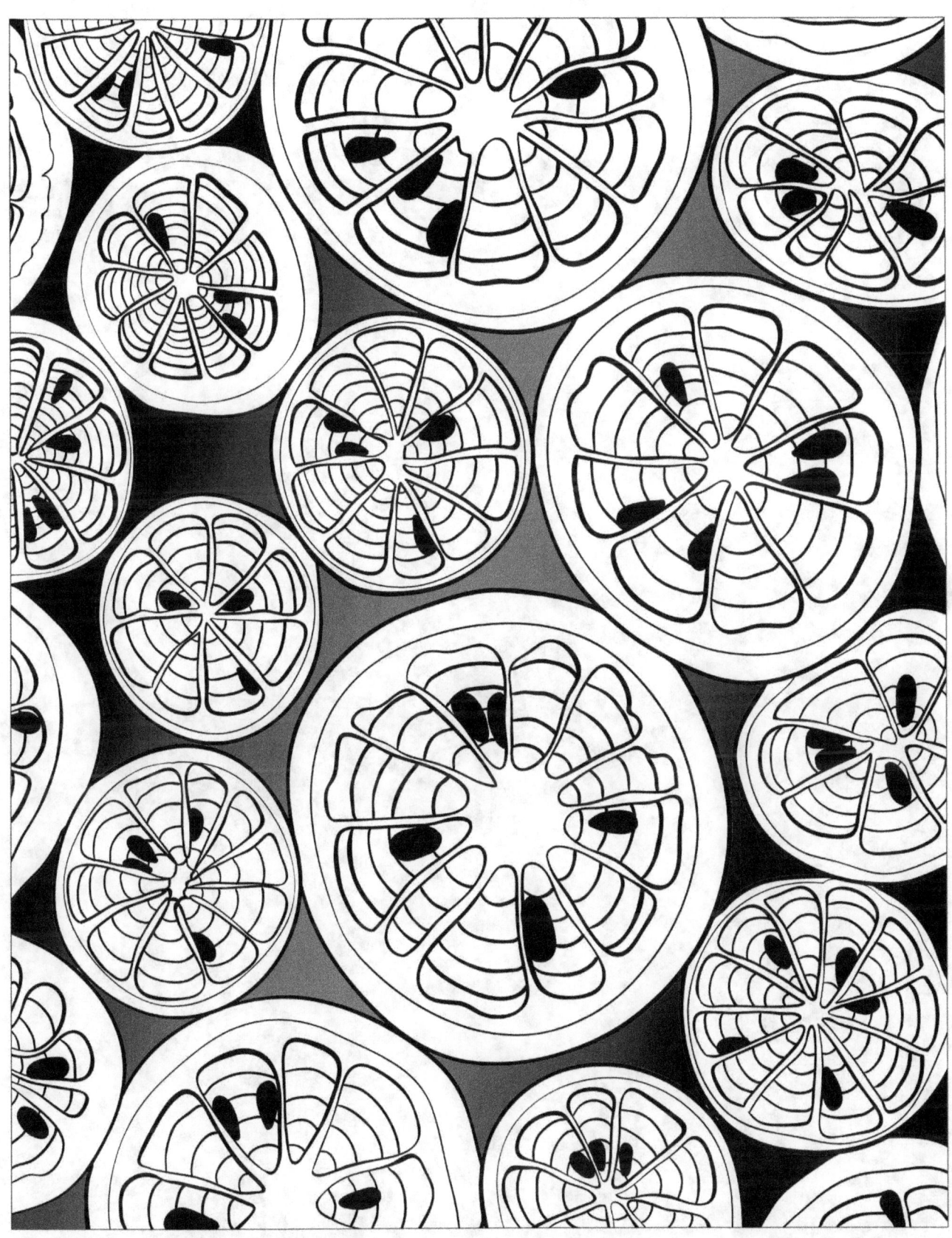

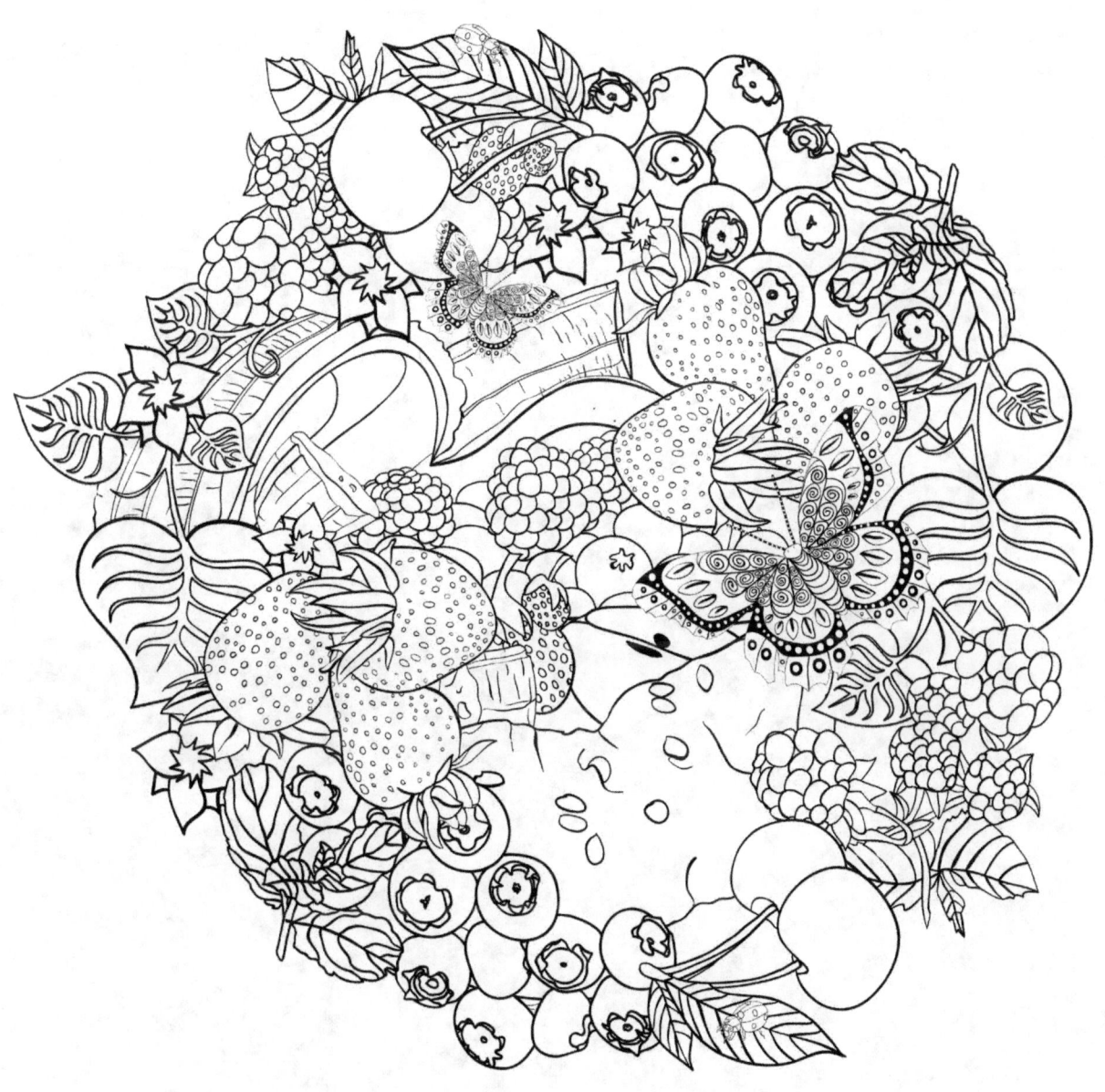

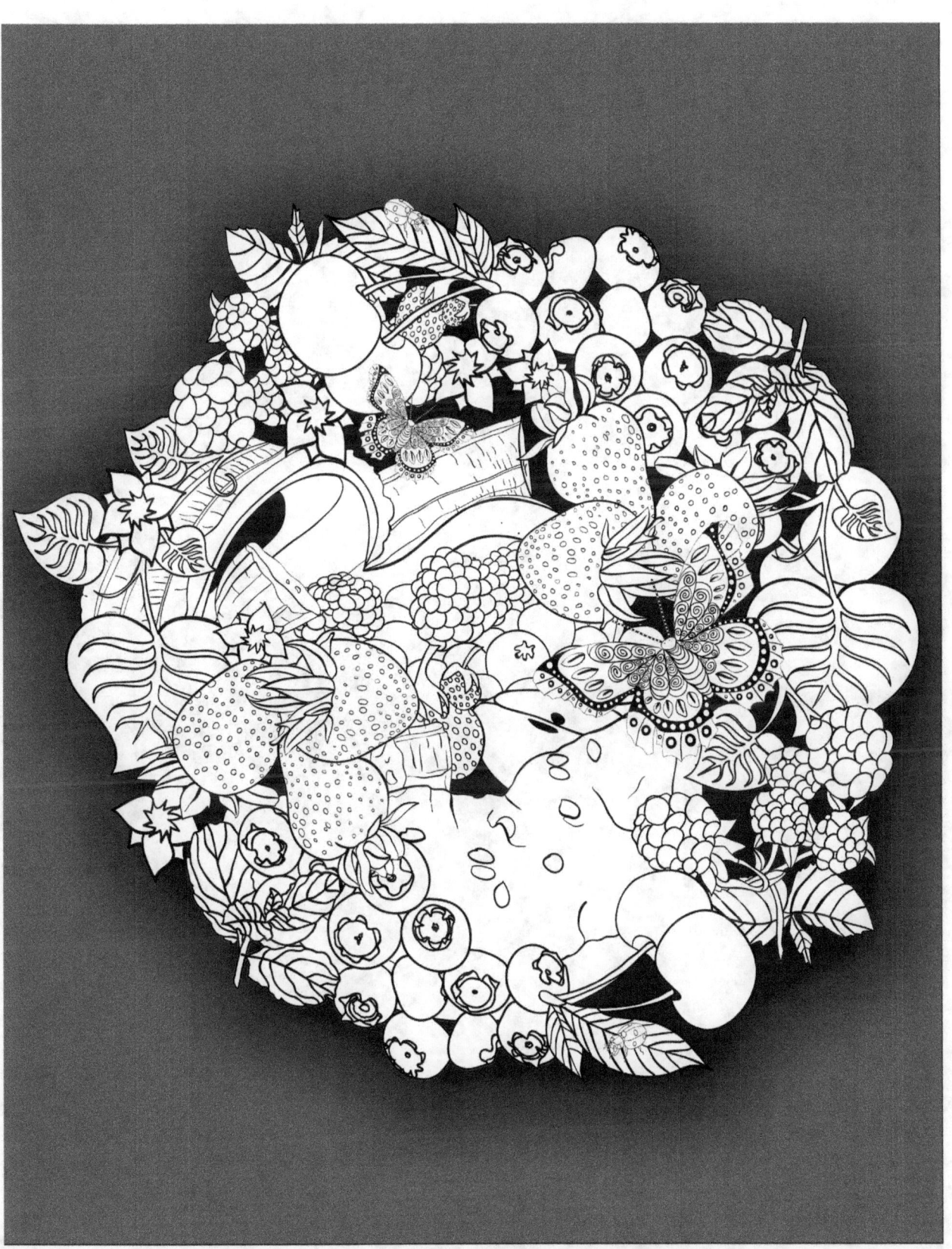

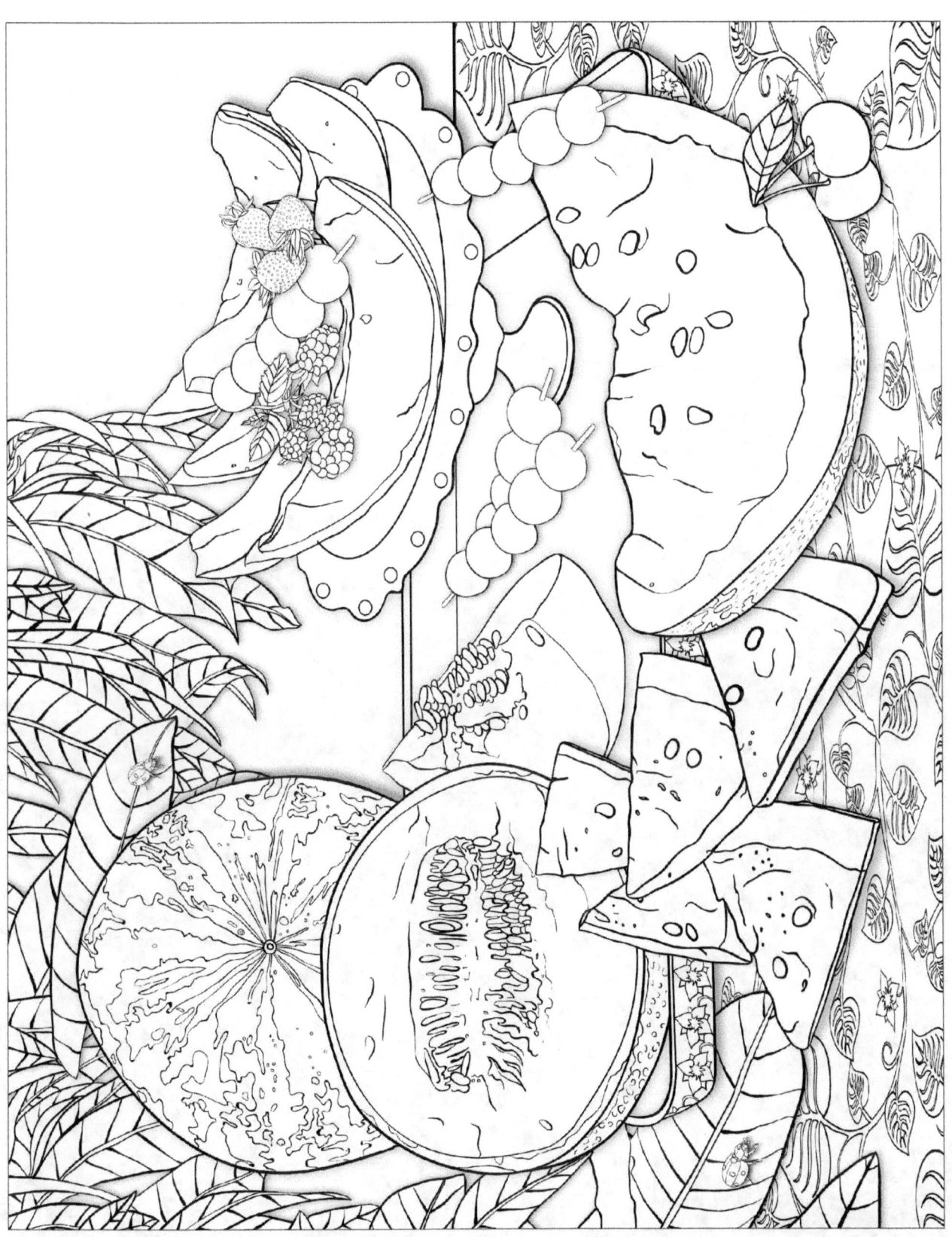

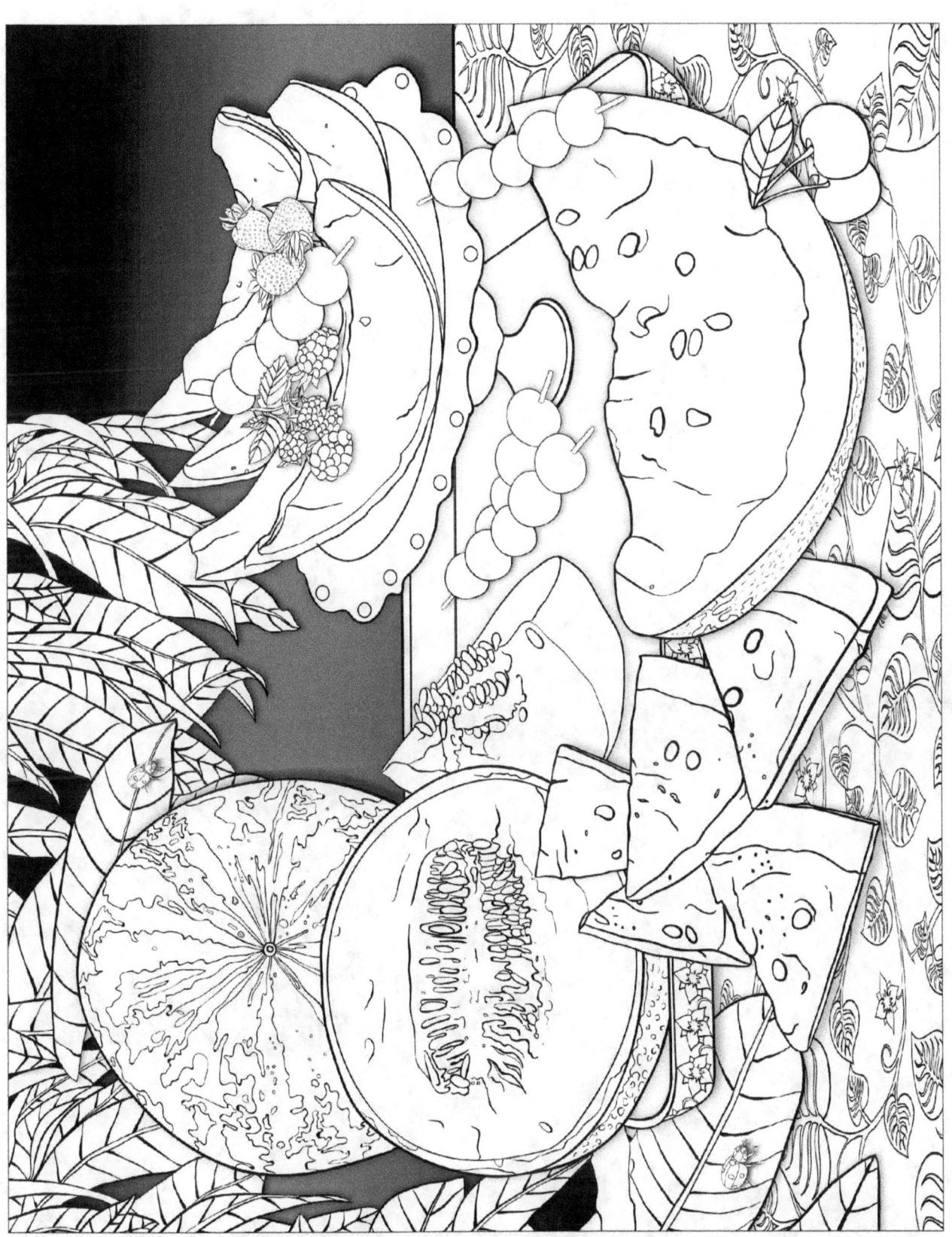

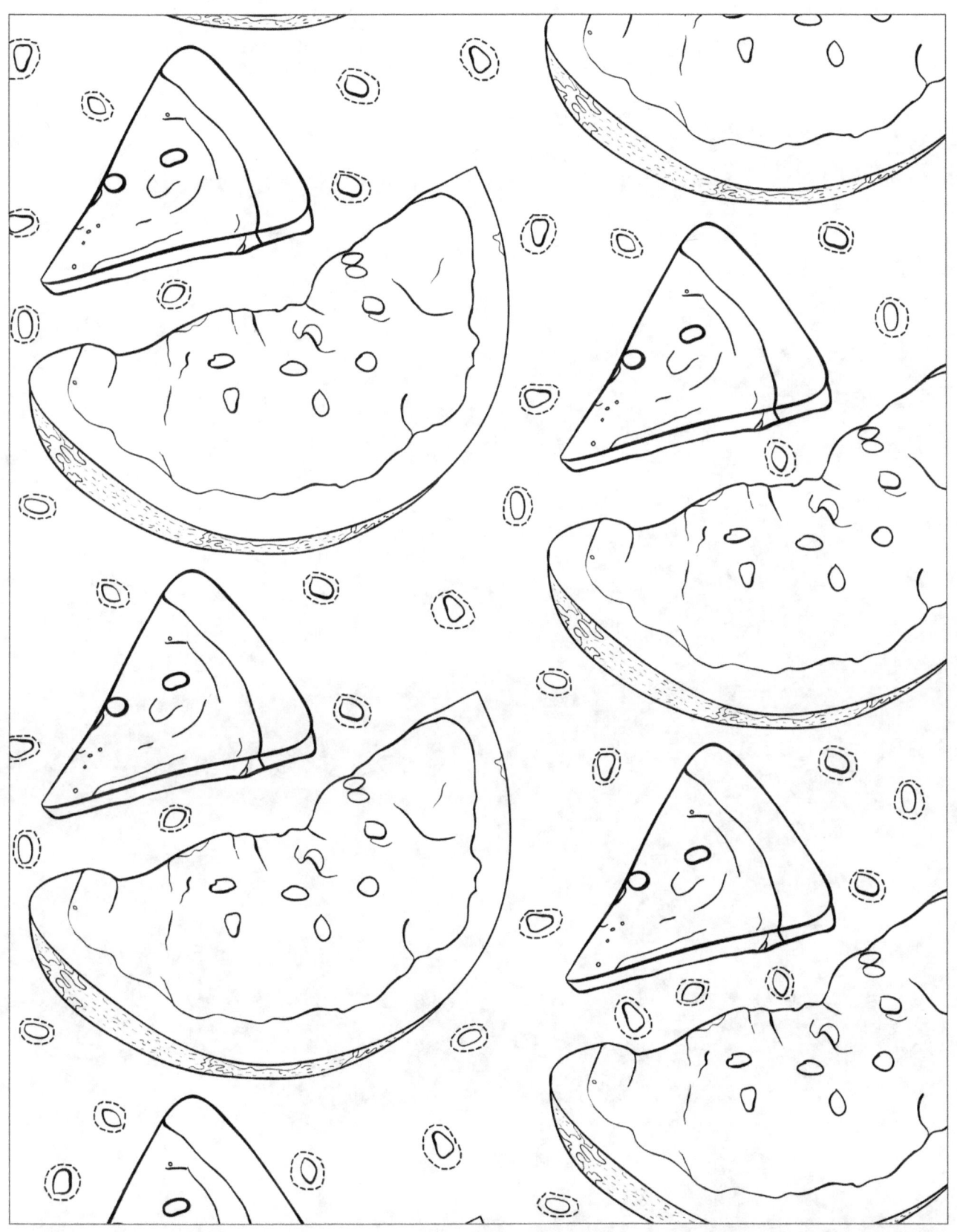

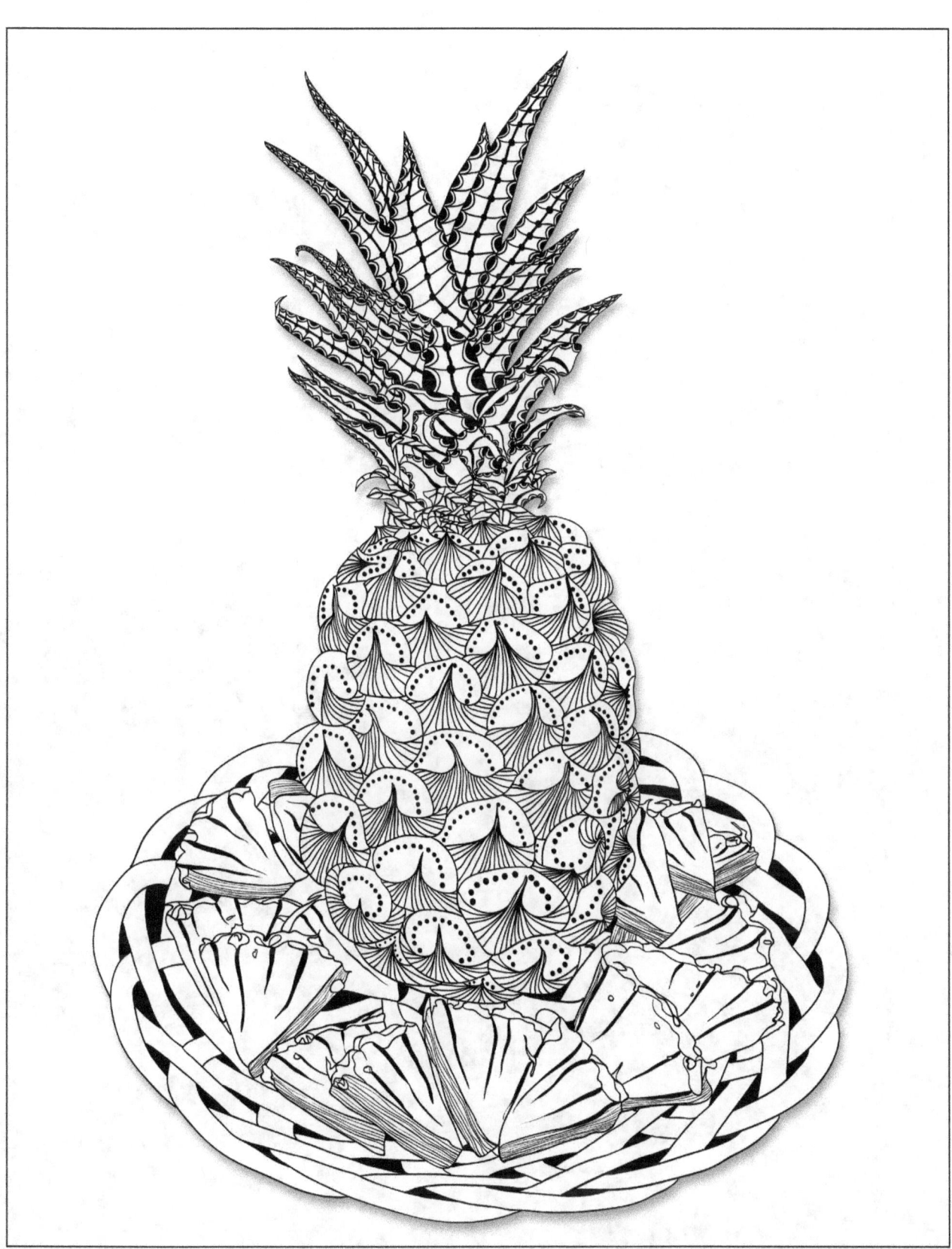

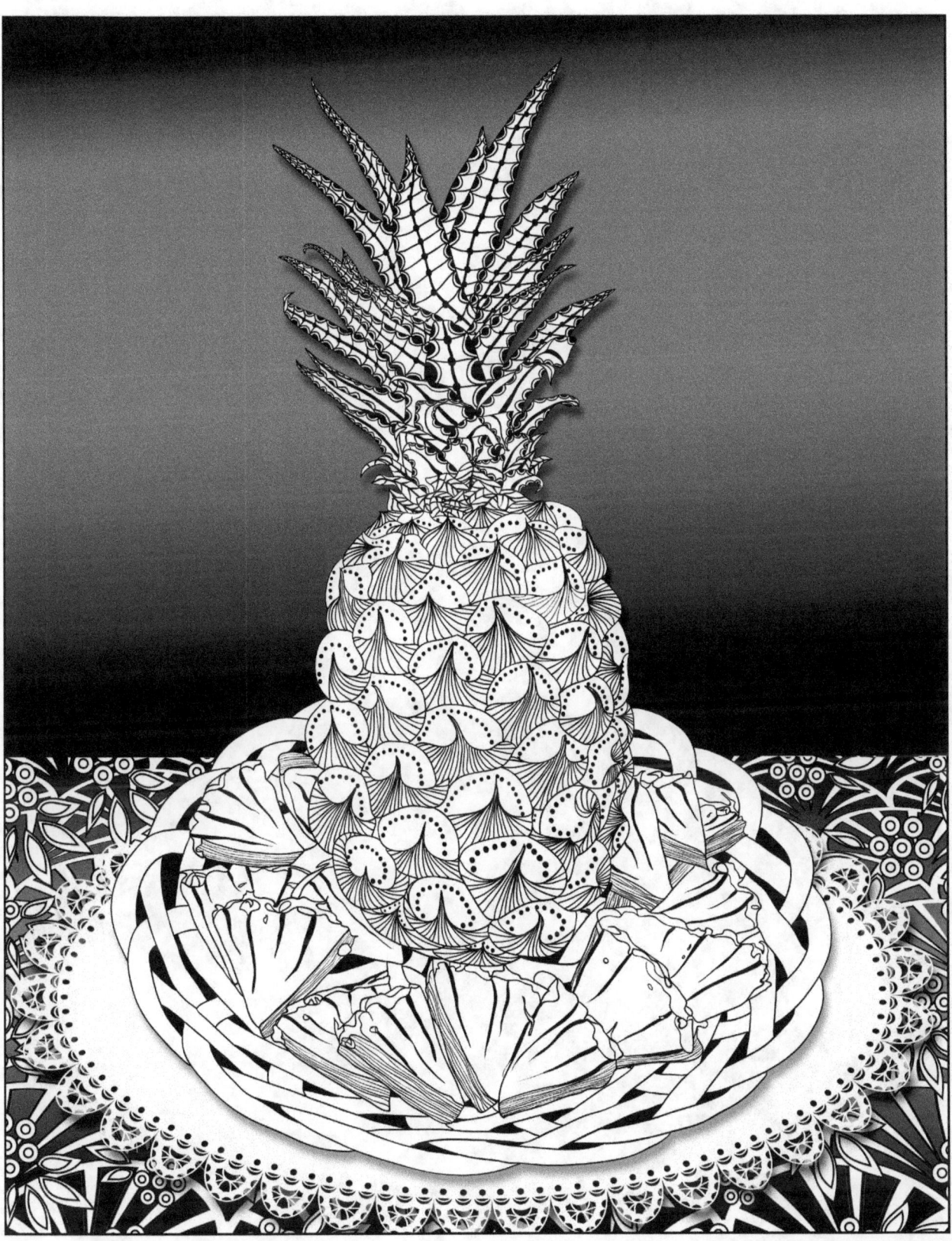

The End

www.ingramcontent.com/pod-product-compliance
Lightning Source LLC
Chambersburg PA
CBHW081256180526

45170CB00007B/2443